D1320593

Wendell Willkie

Willkie at his desk, April 1944. Indiana State Library.

Wendell Willkie

HOOSIER
INTERNATIONALIST

EDITED BY
JAMES H. MADISON

Indiana University Press
Bloomington & Indianapolis

Manufactured in the United States of America

Library of Congress Cataloging-in-Publication Data

Wendell Willkie : Hoosier internationalist / edited by
James H. Madison.
     p.   cm.
     Includes bibliographical references and index.
     ISBN 0-253-33619-8 (alk. paper). — ISBN 0-253-20689-8 (pbk. :
alk. paper)
     1. Willkie, Wendell L. (Wendell Lewis), 1892–1944.
2. Politicians—United States—Biography. 3. Presidential
candidates—United States—Biography. 4. United States—Politics
and government—1933–1945.   I. Madison, James H.
E748.W7W46   1992
973.917'092—dc20
[B]   91-12758

1 2 3 4 5   95 94 93 92 91

CONTENTS

Contents

vi

Illustrations precede Part II.

FOREWORD

Herman B Wells

It is fitting that Indiana University celebrate the hundredth anniversary of Wendell Willkie's birth: he had strong ties to the university, having received three degrees from the institution—AB '13, LLB '16, and LLD '38. When he entered Indiana University on January 4, 1910, two of his brothers and one sister were already here—Herman F., AB '12; Julia E., AB '09, AM '10; and Robert T., AB '09, LLB '11. Julia maintained a house in Bloomington for the clan, and here the lively Willkie tradition of argument, discussion, and serious intellectual debate continued. It was a tradition they had inherited at their home in Elwood, where their father and mother were both attorneys and voracious readers with strong intellectual interests.

Since my baccalaureate was in 1924, I did not overlap with the Willkie era here, but Wendell and his siblings had made such a profound influence on the campus that the traditions of their tenure were still strong in my undergraduate days. But I do well remember when, soon after I became president of the university, Wendell Willkie came to speak at the 1938 Indiana University Foundation Day and to receive an honorary degree. He was already nationally known for his vigorous defense of the private-utility field, which he had represented for some time as a lawyer. In his speech on that spring day, he said:

> So, just as I left the University of Indiana twenty-five years ago, sworn to defend the liberal cause, I return to it today pledged to the same purpose. The liberal cause is still in need of defense. I do not doubt that you will defend it. You could hardly spend four years here in this university, in this state, without absorbing a faith in the rights of man. Perhaps I should warn you, however, that liberalism is neither easy nor sensational. Very rarely is it called upon to storm the barricades with flags waving, and very rarely can it rely simply upon a good heart to determine the merits of its cause. Frequently you will find yourself in the minority, and sometimes you will find yourself alone.
>
> In fact, the liberal attempts to do the most difficult thing in the world—namely, to strike a true balance between the rights of the individual and the needs of society. He is like a man rowing a boat who, when the boat swings to the right pulls on the left, and when it swings to the left, pulls on the right. Liberalism sticks to the middle of the road, speaks quietly and insists upon the color of no man's shirt. If its voice seems small in the present tumult of shouting—if its ranks seem thinned among the regiments in uniform—let that be a sign to you, who have been educated in its spirit, to recognize the urgency of its cause.[1]

After his speech he came to have lunch with me and a few others at Woodburn House. He regaled us with great stories of his recent highly publicized visit with President Franklin Roosevelt in the White House. Although he and Roosevelt were on opposite sides of the private-utility issue, they apparently liked and admired each other. Willkie was a magnetic individual, but his clothes and hair were always slightly rumpled. *Time* wisecracked that he was the only man who could make a four-hundred-dollar suit look like it had come from Macy's bargain basement.

Willkie's return to the campus to make this speech was not surprising, because the entire Willkie family were devoted alumni. From 1938 to 1944, Wendell served as a member of the first Board of Directors of the Indiana University Foundation, organized by alumni to promote the welfare of Indiana University, to stimulate research activity, and to raise money for scholarly pursuits. His brother Herman succeeded him in 1944 and served until 1956. The presidential campaign of 1940 was a lively one. It began with a struggle within the Republican party for the nomination, a struggle that Willkie finally won. Another prominent Republican, a Beta Theta Pi brother and Indiana alumnus, Charles Halleck, managed Willkie's bid for the nomination. I could not attend the great gathering that summer at Elwood, where Willkie formally accepted the nomination of his party, because I was in Mexico. Dr. William Lowe Bryan, Indiana University's retired president, was there and spoke, bringing the university's endorsement and greeting.

In the fall campaign, Willkie had the support of the most progressive elements in the Republican party as well as of quite a few Democrats. William Allen White, a staunch Republican and the social conscience of his party and of America, whose editorials were read and quoted from coast to coast, had this to say in writing to a friend, fellow Republican Justice William A. Smith of the Kansas Supreme Court:

> I'm 100 per cent sold for life on Wendell Willkie and if I am the only man in Kansas who is following him . . . I am going to do it. I have made my living by being a pretty good judge of men, and never since Teddy Roosevelt have I known a man on whom I have pinned my faith as I pinned it on Wendell Willkie. I think one of the most courageous things any man ever said in public life was Willkie's "campaign oratory" statement. It was not discreet, but it was deeply honest. Only three times in public life have I seen such honesty.[2]

All across the country Americans who believed as White believed rallied to the cause of Wendell Willkie.

Although Willkie was defeated in that race, he accepted Roosevelt's invitation to carry a message to the principal leaders of the world that America was still united under its elected president. His talks with the world's leaders on that historic round-the-world mission resulted in his book *One World*, which has had such a profound influence on the thinking of Americans.

At the memorial service conducted by Indiana University a few days after Wendell Willkie's burial at Rushville, Dr. Bryan spoke as follows:

> He died too soon to see realized his dream of One World. He died too soon. But to believe in men in spite of all the evil in them, to believe with all his might that there can be and must be One World of peace, justice, and brotherhood, to have a hope for men akin to Christ's hope for them and to die fighting for it—that is victory. This is the Happy Warrior. This is he, whom every man in arms would wish to be.

While, as Dr. Bryan stated, Willkie died too soon to see his dream realized, events since that time have continued to emphasize the significance and validity of the concept. More and more, business and industry become truly international, political ideas flow freely around the world, and we have literally become, in economic matters at least, one world. The Federation of European Nations to Eliminate All National Boundaries scheduled for 1992 is in a sense a fruit of Willkie's dream. More and more we realize that we are one world and that his book, *One World,* is prophetic in its vision. We must have either one world or none.

Wendell Willkie occupies a unique place in the alumni annals of Indiana University: he is the only graduate to be nominated for the presidency. The ideas he presented to the world are alive, constantly renewed by events and helping to shape the world of the future.

NOTES

1. Willkie's Foundation Day Address is reprinted at the end of this collection.
2. William Allen White, *The Autobiography of William Allen White* (New York, 1946), 645. Willkie predicted in a campaign speech that FDR would

have the nation at war by April 1941. Questioned by Senator Gerald P. Nye, an isolationist, about the statement, Willkie answered, "It was a bit of campaign oratory." In Steve Neal, *Dark Horse: A Biography of Wendell Willkie* (Garden City, N.Y., 1984), p. 206.

THINKING ABOUT
WENDELL WILLKIE

AN INTRODUCTION

James H. Madison

Across much of the American republic during the weekend of October 7–8, 1944, a lovely Indian summer sun momentarily hid the harsh winter to come. In St. Louis two hometown teams, the Cardinals and the Browns, struggled to win the World Series with a collection of mostly older, castoff players (none of them black, of course, in those days before Jackie Robinson). The War Department released the new casualty report from overseas, a list of 2,648 names. In their Sunday morning newspapers Americans read of the latest air raid over Germany, in which 5,500 Allied planes hurled ten thousand tons of bombs on the Nazi war machine. And they read of the presidential campaign of challenger Thomas E. Dewey to unseat President Franklin D. Roosevelt, who was seeking an unprecedented fourth term in the White House.

But the most shocking news that Sunday morning was that Wendell Willkie had died. He was only fifty-two, the victim of a heart attack. Amid the disbelief and sorrow there was a sense not only of personal tragedy but also of national loss, especially now, as a *New York Times* reporter lamented, when this man was so clearly needed for the approaching postwar world.

Five decades later Willkie's life and early death raise poignantly the "what if" question: what if he had lived his allotted three score and ten? What influence might he have had in the Cold War that followed the peace of 1945? What role might he have played in the slow and painful march toward civil rights for African Americans? Thinking about Willkie nearly a half century after his death and one hundred years after his birth brings such questions quickly to mind.

The seven original essays in this collection do not deal directly with these questions. All the essayists are serious, professional historians, and none is so foolhardy as to engage in counterfactual speculation, at least in print. That thoughtful readers of these essays will doubtless find such questions rumbling through their heads, however, constitutes powerful testimony to the large and lasting significance of Wendell Willkie. The record of his life, and particularly of its last four years, provides abundant evidence that here was a man who made a difference, a man whose vision and insight into his time and place were powerful and unique, making the tragedy of his early death all the more poignant. On two matters especially Willkie made enduring contributions: in his advanced views on the international responsibilities that now confronted the United States and in his impassioned appeal for justice and equality of opportunity for African Americans.

Wendell Willkie was born in Elwood, Indiana, on February 18, 1892. The *New York Times* later described him as "a former Indiana farm boy," but that label is misleading. His German-American parents were both lawyers, and in the Willkie home reading and discussion of books were the norm, not farm chores or talk of corn prices. Books were a constant in his life, in fact, and he read with an appetite unusual for someone who so intensely liked the company of people. Growing up in Elwood, Willkie attended the local high school, where his successes came on the debate team and as senior class president. At Indiana University in Bloomington he flirted with socialism before settling down as a liberal Democrat and enthusiastic supporter of Woodrow Wilson, another bookish sort. After graduation in 1913 Willkie moved to Kansas and briefly taught high school history, a subject he always loved. He later claimed that he really wanted above all else to be a college history professor. He soon returned to Bloomington to earn a law degree, however, then joined his father's law practice in Elwood. With American entry into World War I in 1917 Willkie joined the army, and before shipping overseas to France he married Edith Wilk, a librarian from Rushville, Indiana. After the war the Willkies moved to Akron, Ohio, where he accepted a position in the legal department of Firestone Tire and Rubber. He later moved to an Akron law firm and specialized in public utilities. He also took an active part in Democratic party politics in Akron. From this point on he returned to Indiana only for short visits, but as George T. Blakey shows in his essay in this collection, "Willkie as a Hoosier," the Indiana years and Hoosier ties remained a formative and enduring part of his life.

Willkie's appearance on the national political stage began after he moved to New York City in 1929 to do legal work for Commonwealth and Southern, a huge public utilities holding company. Rising quickly, he became president of Commonwealth and Southern in 1933, the same year Franklin Roosevelt entered the White House. Almost immediately the two men were locked in a political battle that raised Willkie to wide recognition as one of the most articulate critics of Roosevelt's New Deal. Willkie thought of himself as a liberal, as he indicated in his Foundation Day speech at Indiana University in 1938, but the shifting political environment of the 1930s made his political life considerably more complex than any simple label could convey. Mark Leff's essay, "Strange Bedfellows," sorts out the Depression era's labyrinthine politics to show how this small-town Hoosier Democrat evolved from spokesman for Republican businessmen to presidential candidate.

Willkie's decision to seek the presidency in 1940 produced one of the most exciting political quests in American history. At a time when Republicans often were thought of as stodgy, stiff, and narrow-minded, Willkie burst on the scene with a charisma and appeal unmatched in his party since the days of Theodore Roosevelt. His plain, direct manner in speech and dress touched a chord with millions of Americans. "There was about him," the *New York Times*

editorialized, "a warm and winning sincerity, an almost boyish ex-
uberance of spirit and a natural straightforwardness which left un-
touched no one who knew him."[1] Often he sat in a chair with one
leg thrown over the arm. His suit was usually rumpled, his hair
falling over his forehead. In conversation and debate he was energetic, witty, and warm, with a genuine intellectual curiosity and a
sense of the dramatic that went back to his declamations of Shake-
speare in the Elwood family parlor. In New York Willkie lived mod-
estly despite his hefty Wall Street salary. He did not own an
automobile because he found taxis more convenient. Until the 1940
campaign heated up he and Edith had only one telephone in their
Fifth Avenue apartment, and it was located in the pantry. They
entertained only infrequently and had no nearby weekend retreat;
Willkie preferred an evening or weekend at home alone, reading.
He could and did occasionally get away to Indiana; by 1940 he
owned five farms near Rushville. Willkie made no pretense of being
a farmer, however. He farmed, he told one interviewer, "by conversation."[2]

Willkie's openness with the press won him admirers among journalists. Unlike many politicians, he genuinely enjoyed bantering
with reporters, as he smoked his Camel cigarettes and sometimes
talked of one day owning his own newspaper. "It was his habit,"
one reporter recalled, "to talk with us frankly on almost any prov-
ocation, to disclose his real opinions of men and affairs without the
caution and reserve which mark so many public men."[3]

His closest associate among journalists was Irita Van Doren, who
edited the book review section of the *New York Herald Tribune*.
Smart and articulate, Van Doren played a major role in Willkie's
intellectual and political growth. Often she helped him to frame his
ideas and communicate them in speeches and articles. There was
more than political spark between the two: they soon became lovers,
passionately devoted to each other, emotionally and intellectually.
She was, Willkie told her, the woman "I admire inordinately and
love excessively."[4] His relationship with Van Doren was widely
known among journalists and others but was never reported in the
press. Edith Willkie surely knew but bore the burden privately, joining her husband on the arduous campaign trail.

Willkie's nomination for the presidency at the Philadelphia convention and his acceptance speech in Elwood were the high points of the 1940 campaign, as Ross Gregory explains in his essay "Seeking the Presidency." Both occasions demonstrated the intense appeal of the candidate, with 150,000 people making their way to Elwood to hear him speak on an August day when the thermometer topped one hundred degrees—the kind of heat, Hoosiers always said, that allowed them to hear the corn grow. Thereafter, Roosevelt's continuing popularity and unparalleled political skills combined with the war in Europe to make Willkie's quest for the White House increasingly difficult. Willkie's strengths as candidate were not in the day-to-day toil of professional politics, even though he waged one of the most aggressive and energetic campaigns in history. One journalist later described the Willkie campaign as "the most disorganized, planless campaign the country has ever seen, . . . a series of blunders and frantic disorganization."[5] Nonetheless, although FDR beat him soundly, Willkie won more popular votes in 1940 than any previous Republican candidate.

Defeated presidential candidates often slump to political exile and popular obscurity. Willkie not only remained in the center of the public eye after his loss but also rendered genuine service to his country. His voice rang loudly in international and domestic affairs during the years from 1940 to 1944. In these years, too, there was considerable evidence of his capacity for intellectual and political growth: "He was a man," the Manchester *Guardian* reported, "who was always learning."[6]

Much of Willkie's growth and most visible service came in arguing the case for internationalism. To label Willkie a Hoosier internationalist might seem an oxymoron. Hoosiers and midwesterners in general were widely and sometimes correctly perceived to be provincial, isolated by geography and culture from the New York–Washington corridor and from the world beyond America's shores. In the 1930s and early 1940s *Midwest* and *isolationism* seemed almost synonymous terms, shouted most vigorously in the bullhorn voice of Colonel Robert McCormick's *Chicago Tribune*. Moreover, it was the Republican party, with its foundation deep in the American heartland, that gave isolationism its most potent political expression. With his roots set in Hoosier soil and his political fortunes cast with the GOP, Willkie might seem the least likely candidate to lead a campaign for internationalism. Yet, as the essays in the second part of this collection make forcefully clear, such was in fact the case.

In "One World: An American Perspective," Howard Jones analyzes the Hoosier Republican's important contributions in moving the United States away from isolationism, contributions, Jones argues, that were second only to those of Roosevelt. In fact, one of Willkie's handicaps in the 1940 race, some thought, was his close agreement with Roosevelt in favor of aiding the Allied powers against Nazi Germany. Willkie's sympathies lodged forcefully with Britain. He actively supported lend-lease aid and soon after the election, in early 1941, made a highly publicized goodwill visit to that war-torn nation, carrying a letter from Roosevelt to Winston Churchill. Willkie's most famous trip, however, came in late summer 1942. This journey around the world included meetings with leaders in the Middle East, the Soviet Union, and China—at a time when long-distance travel by political figures and shuttle diplomacy were little practiced. On his return to the United States he addressed, over all four radio networks, an audience estimated at thirty-six million people. "In the rumble of that heavy midwestern voice," the *Christian Century* reported, Willkie raised "a battle cry for freedom."[7] "There are no distant points in the world any longer," he told his listeners. Ideas such as freedom also travel in this small world, he warned, and hopes rise for independence in the Mideast and places such as India, still struggling under the yoke of colonialism. And, Willkie told his audience, it was not sufficient simply to win the war; America must win the peace, too, by promoting international cooperation and justice and freedom, abroad and at home.[8]

Popular interest in Willkie's trip around the world and encouragement from Van Doren and others pushed him to write a book. *One World* appeared in April 1943. In clear and sprightly prose, Willkie provided evidence from his trip to support his assertion that "our thinking must be world-wide."[9] The book sold more than a million copies in two months and a second million before the year was over. According to a statement made at the time by the publisher, Simon and Schuster, "No book in the history of book publishing has been bought by so many people so quickly."[10] Critics lauded Willkie's achievement. William L. Shirer called it "one of the most absorbing books I have read in years," noting that Willkie's "exuberant personality fairly bubbles" from every page.[11] The reactions of two of America's best writers, both with Indiana roots, suggest the breadth of appeal of *One World*. Booth Tarkington, a traditionalist and a Republican, praised the book as "written with a breathless honesty" by a man who "has personally experienced the small roundness of the 20th century world."[12] Theodore Dreiser, a more curmudgeonly and radical Hoosier author, also joined in the praise, writing Willkie to commend him "on your courage" in addressing the "powder keg" represented by the aspirations of common people throughout the world.[13] Willkie was not an infallible prophet, of course; as André Kaspi notes in his essay in this collection, *One World* provides evidence of Willkie's shortsightedness as well as his farsighted vision in assessing America's place in a rapidly changing world. More cynical critics might even ask whether Willkie's internationalism was partly a design to open the world to American business and thereby build a new kind of economic imperialism to replace the dying colonialism of the European powers. Still, even a half century after its publication, *One World* remains a book worthy of reading and pondering.

Not everyone liked *One World*. The *Chicago Tribune* Sunday book review section damned it with a skimpy, page-twelve review, no accompanying pictures, and a dismissal of the author as a simpleminded tourist whose major arguments were unworthy of discussion.[14] More sustained negative attention appeared in a mocking pamphlet, *One Man—Wendell Willkie*, written by C. Nelson Sparks, a midwestern Republican who claimed that the book represented "the planned conspiracy of the New Dealers and the Willkie internationalists to force the United States into an acceptance of a permanent union of world government with Europe and Asia." Willkie was nothing more than "a New Deal 'fellow traveler,'" Sparks charged, a politician who used "sucker-bait phrases, [like] 'One

World,' 'brotherhood of man,' 'workers of the world,' and 'all God's children.' "[15] Willkie suffered increasingly strong criticism from within his own party, particularly from professionals and the conservative Old Guard who had always regarded him as an outsider and had never accepted his internationalism or his stubborn independence. Nonetheless, he pushed and pushed within the party, with some effect, as Alexander Manykin shows in his essay in this collection.

Willkie also began to think beyond the Republican party, particularly after it denied him any role in the 1944 campaign. He and Roosevelt had often locked horns, but as James MacGregor Burns noted, they had "a sneaking affection for each other."[16] By 1944 there was even some consideration of joining with Roosevelt to form a third party, one in which Willkie would be free of the Republican Old Guard and FDR would be liberated from the conservative southern wing of his Democratic party. The death of both men within six months left another of those "what if" questions.

Willkie's forward stand on internationalism was more than matched by his views on racial equality. In an age when segregation, discrimination, and inequality were commonplace for African Americans everywhere, North and South, Willkie spoke passionately for justice and equality. As Harvard Sitkoff argues in his essay "Willkie as Liberal," this man who grew up in a time and place that paid scant attention to racial justice came by the early 1940s to a position that was two decades ahead of most of his contemporaries. Willkie developed a close working relationship with Walter White, head of the National Association for the Advancement of Colored People, and sent part of his royalties from the sale of *One World* to the NAACP Legal Defense and Education Fund. More important, Willkie used his access to the communications media to write and speak on the issue of race, doing so with a frequency and a conviction that few if any nationally known white Americans of the 1940s could match. He argued strongly and with some effect, for example, that Hollywood filmmakers indulged in highly biased portrayals of African Americans. And in a radio address on race hatred in July 1943, he asserted that all Americans, including black Americans, had a right to decent housing: "If this cannot be secured through the operation of our private economy, it is an obligation that must be undertaken by government—preferably local, but if necessary, federal."[17]

Always Willkie was careful to point not only to the pressing questions of justice at home but also to those abroad, linking the struggle of American blacks to the struggles against colonialism and racism overseas. In an address to the 1942 NAACP convention Willkie noted that "when we talk of freedom and opportunity for all nations the mocking paradoxes of our own society become so clear they can no longer be ignored."[18] These views were not popular with foreign leaders such as Churchill nor with many white Americans at home, among them the Louisiana supporter who encouraged Willkie to run for the presidency in 1944 but warned him to "lay off this equality project."[19] Even Willkie's friends and admirers seem not to have fully appreciated the significance of his progressive views on race.[20] Not surprising, but worthy of comment in the press at the time of Willkie's death, was the large number of African-American mourners in the long lines that stretched outside the Fifth Avenue Presbyterian Church.

The world moved quickly after Willkie's death on that Indian summer weekend in 1944. Some people tried aggressively to forget him; in many quarters there was what his friend Joseph Barnes later remembered as "the great silence." The 1948 Republican convention, for example, contained the usual quota of long and forgettable speeches, none of which mentioned Willkie.[21] In the atmosphere of Cold War and then McCarthyism there seemed less room for Willkie's optimistic internationalism or his progressive notions of racial equality. He was remembered, if at all, as the dark-horse candidate with tousled hair and rumpled suit, a flash in the pan in a long-past political season.

And yet to a later generation—one that has seen the struggles for civil rights of the 1960s, the collapse of colonialism and the emergence of new nations, the clanging fall of the Iron Curtain—to this generation there is reason to remember and to consider: what if Willkie had lived beyond his fifty-two years? Would he have helped soften Cold War anxieties about the Soviet Union? Would he have brought greater understanding and sympathy to the struggles against colonialism in Asia, Africa, and the Mideast? Would he have resisted the McCarthyism that cowered much of his party and nation? Would he have responded more vigorously to the pleas of African Americans, including those from the black family in Topeka, Kansas, in the early 1950s who wanted only for their child to attend the neighborhood school? Perhaps.

Even without such fanciful exercises in counterfactual history there is good reason to examine what this man actually did and said in a life too brief, from his Hoosier origins, through his Wall Street career, to his presidential campaign, to his quest for internationalism and racial justice. The essays that follow provide the reader with abundant opportunity to read and to think.

These essays are the work of many hands. They originated in the mind of Herman B Wells, chancellor of Indiana University, who wished to celebrate the centennial of Wendell Willkie's birth and who kindly agreed to write a foreword for the collection that would highlight Willkie's attachment to the university. Indiana University President Thomas Ehrlich enthusiastically supported the project. The largest thanks goes to the authors, of course, who produced their essays with a skill and care that considerably lessened the editor's tasks. Each essay was written to stand alone, and that has resulted in some overlap and repetition; but the collection together, we hope, provides the basis for a fuller understanding of this extraordinary man. I am indebted also to Bhavna Dave, who translated the essay written in Russian, and Barbara Brady Pieroni, who did the French translation. Valuable assistance has also been received from Saundra Taylor, who cares for the Willkie Papers in Indiana University's Lilly Library. Several colleagues in the History Department at Indiana have also helped, including William Cohen, Ben Eklof, Michael McGerr, and John Wilz. To all these people I express my gratitude for making this book possible and for helping me become better acquainted with this intriguing Hoosier internationalist.

NOTES

1. *New York Times,* October 9, 1944.
2. Janet Flanner, "Rushville's Renowned Son-in-Law," *New Yorker,* October 12, 1940, 34.
3. Roscoe Drummond, "Wendell Willkie: A Study in Courage," in Isabel Leighton, ed., *The Aspirin Age, 1919–1941* (New York, 1949), 449.
4. Wendell Willkie to Irita Van Doren, n.d., box 10, Irita Van Doren Papers, Library of Congress, Washington, D.C. Van Doren's large contribution to Willkie's speeches and writings is evident in her papers. See, for example, "Speech, 1943," box 21, Van Doren Papers. See also Steve Neal, *Dark Horse: A Biography of Wendell Willkie* (Garden City, N.Y., 1984), 37–44, and Ellsworth Barnard, "Postscript to *Wendell Willkie: Fighter for Freedom,*" Ellsworth Barnard Papers, Lilly Library, Indiana University, Bloomington. Barnard provided a detailed assessment of the evidence regarding the Willkie–Van Doren relationship; he did not, however, have access to the Van Doren Papers.
5. *Detroit Free Press,* October 15, 1944.
6. Quoted in *New York Times,* October 9, 1944.
7. *Christian Century,* November 4, 1942, 1343, 1344.
8. "Report to the People, October 26, 1942," Speeches/Writing Files, Wendell Willkie Papers, Lilly Library, Indiana University, Bloomington.
9. Wendell L. Willkie, *One World* (New York, 1943), 2.
10. Advertisement in *Life,* July 12, 1943.
11. William L. Shirer, review, *New York Herald Tribune Weekly Book Review,* April 11, 1943, 1.
12. *Indianapolis Star,* April 11, 1943.
13. Theodore Dreiser to Wendell Willkie, June 28, 1944, box 23, Willkie Papers.
14. *Chicago Tribune Book Review,* April 11, 1943, 12.
15. C. Nelson Sparks, *One Man—Wendell Willkie* (New York, 1943), 47, 46.
16. James MacGregor Burns, *Roosevelt: The Soldier of Freedom* (New York, 1970), 274.
17. Wendell Willkie, "Race Hatred Broadcast," July 1943, box 21, Van Doren Papers. See also *Pittsburgh Courier,* October 14, 1944, which called

Willkie "the greatest champion of their [African Americans'] cause in modern times."

18. Quoted in Ellsworth Barnard, *Wendell Willkie: Fighter for Freedom* (Marquette, Mich., 1966), 340.

19. Henry A. Mentz to Willkie, August 8, 1943, Personal Correspondence, Willkie Papers.

20. See, for example, Drummond, "Wendell Willkie," 444–75, an otherwise perceptive essay by an admiring reporter that does not mention the issue of race.

21. Joseph Barnes, *Willkie* (New York, 1952), 388–89.

PART I

Wendell Willkie in Indiana & America

GEORGE T. BLAKEY

Willkie as a Hoosier

FROM ELWOOD TO RUSHVILLE
AND IN BETWEEN

WENDELL L. WILLKIE's credentials as a Hoosier are deep and broad. They need little explanation for him to be accepted into the Indiana pantheon of distinguished native sons. Born and raised in Elwood, educated at Indiana University, married to a native daughter, resident of the state for more than half his life, and buried in Rushville, he possesses numerous valid claims to Hoosierdom. Furthermore, Teutonic blood from grandparents on both sides of his family gave him a direct link to a major chapter of Indiana history. German immigrants constituted the largest ethnic bloc of the state population and had been instrumental in the growth of several Hoosier cities, including Fort Wayne, Richmond, Evansville, and Indianapolis. Various symbolic relationships also enhanced Willkie's status as a Hoosier. As a successful businessman he represented free enterprise principles so dear to the Indiana economy, and as a presidential candidate he reflected the Hoosier obsession with politics. In many respects Willkie was Indiana personified.

Despite these obvious connections to Hoosier soil and symbolism, Willkie's identity as a native son is, nevertheless, clouded. During his lifetime many Hoosiers argued that he was neither typical of them nor a good representative symbol of the state. His conscious choice to leave Indiana was one of their main arguments. He had indeed left the state shortly after becoming an adult, and his physical links with Indiana in the latter half of his life were brief stopovers or vacations with his wife's family. Compounding this argument was his own admission that the best time of his life was the decade he lived in Akron, Ohio, from 1919 to 1929. The great fame and wealth that Willkie attained came only during his fifteen-year residence in New York, from 1929 to 1944. Most Americans knew him as a corporation president, opponent of President Franklin D. Roosevelt's New Deal, and candidate for the White House, none of which had roots in Hoosier soil. And as an articulate spokesman for liberal ideas, internationalism, and equality for minorities, Willkie supplied strong evidence for those who denied his claims to Hoosierdom. Indiana and conservatism were almost synonymous, isolationism was deeply ingrained in the state's world outlook, and Indiana's record regarding racial and religious minorities was not an enlightened one. Both physically and intellectually Willkie lived a long distance from the land of his birth.

These deviations from the Hoosier norm, undeniable as they were, cannot prevent Wendell Willkie from ultimately being regarded as a son of Indiana. In at least four significant ways he represented the state and the Hoosier character in an exemplary fashion. His perpetuation of the rural Indiana myth, his fierce independence from outside pressure, his abilities as an orator, and his accomplishments as a writer all place him in the mainstream of Hoosier tradition. An examination of these four characteristics will illustrate that the man and the state were wedded inextricably.

In the autumn of 1943, Wendell L. Willkie had been living at a deluxe address in Manhattan for more than a dozen years, was the author of a best-selling book concerning international relations, was a wealthy and successful lawyer, a former candidate for the presidency of the United States, and the recent president of a major utilities firm. In his leisure time he cultivated the company of an elite literary circle or enjoyed the Broadway theater. Here, by his own choice, was an urban and urbane citizen of the world. Yet that autumn *Look* magazine ran a major story about him with a cover portrait of a slightly disheveled gentry farmer; behind him, stretching into agricultural infinity, were acres of lush cropland in the manner of a Renaissance landscape. That same season, an article in the *New Republic* depicted Willkie as "a rumple-haired simple-hearted boy from Indiana."[1] This glaring contradiction of images, this portrayal of a Penrod in pinstripes, had become a journalist's staple. It represented a nostalgic vision of Willkie's rural past and a denial of the urban realities of the present. Half-truths and distortions, these images were popular and were done with Willkie's consent and cooperation.

Portrayals of Willkie as the bucolic hayseed began before his presidential candidacy in 1940, then intensified. Writers had emphasized the quaint origins of the powerful president of Commonwealth and Southern as he fought against the federal government in the 1930s. An "Indiana crackerbox debater in store clothes," *Time* had called him.[2] Following his nomination for the presidency, *Newsweek* described the site of his forthcoming acceptance speech, Elwood's Callaway Park, as the place "where he used to splash in the old swimmin' hole. . . ."[3] Any reader who failed to recognize this aquatic reference to Hoosier poet James Whitcomb Riley would have had less difficulty with the parody run by the *New Yorker* later that year. MacKinlay Kantor's "Back Home in Indyanner" threw all subtlety aside and bowdlerized Riley's verse to caricature Willkie:

> He's 'ist as plain as plain can be;
> He never combs his hair;
> He loves th' oldest slippers
> An' the quaintest rockin' chair.[4]

Photographers who accompanied Willkie to Indiana during his campaign trips invariably sought opportunities to picture the candidate against backgrounds of crops and livestock. One observer quipped that Hoosier hogs grew so accustomed to this routine they would strike poses whenever photographers approached.

What is especially ironic about these sylvan images is that Wendell Willkie spent his entire life in urban settings, with a rare summer stint of farm labor as a youth. The Elwood of his childhood was a raucous industrial city whose huge tinplate and glass factories had benefited from the natural gas boom of the 1880s. The young Willkie spent one summer toiling in the noise and heat of one of the tinplate plants. Neither was Willkie's frame of reference at all rural. Elwood had paved streets and a library and a generous share of bars and brothels. When the shopping opportunities there did not satisfy his mother, she would hustle her children off to Chicago to buy their clothes at Marshall Field's department store. Following his education at Bloomington and his military service in France during the Great War, Willkie soon moved to Akron, a boom city on a greater scale than Elwood's. Its population during his decade there exeeded two hundred thousand. Of all the residences that Willkie called home, perhaps the only one with any claim to pastoral charm was his apartment in New York; just across Fifth Avenue was Central Park. Furthermore, Willkie was not a farmer, even if he owned approximately fifteen hundred acres of farmland in Rush County, Indiana. These farms were purchased as an investment, managed by an overseer, and worked by tenants. Willkie frequently affirmed that he had never farmed and vowed that he did not intend to. Hoosier author John Bartlow Martin correctly assessed Willkie's tenuous connection to agricultural life in Rush County with another Rileyesque allusion: "Hoosiers knew [Willkie's] acreage belonged to no poor farmer, . . . here farming is a capitalist's enterprise, not a raggedy man's."[5]

Verbal and visual deception that it was, Willkie played along with this presentation of him as the hayseed-come-to-town. This deception bore tangible benefits. During his quest for the Republican presidential nomination he wanted to appear less of a Wall Street habitué and more of a Main Street American. For a fund raiser he permitted some Indiana University alumni in New York to organize an old-fashioned box supper with decorations simulating a little red schoolhouse. This, supposedly, would help to remove the stigma of being an eastern business magnate. Willkie also sought and used the blessing of his literary idol, Hoosier Booth Tarkington, whose reputation for glorifying small-town virtues ranked almost as high as Riley's. Tarkington assessed Willkie as "a man wholly natural in manner, a man with no pose, no 'swellness,' no condescension, . . . a good, sturdy, plain, able Hoosier. . . . "⁶ In keeping with this endorsement, Willkie would ruffle himself before being photographed and admit that in his line of work it was best to look like an Indiana farmer. Although he drew the line at being photographed in overalls or on a tractor, he often reminded voters in the Midwest that thirty-seven of his forty-eight years had been spent in the agrarian heartland, that he had worked in the fields as a college student, and that he had never really lost touch with the land. Willkie effectively resurrected a rural past for political gain, even though the past in question was more myth than fact.

Willkie was willing to be an accessory to the making of this rural myth mainly for political reasons. The United States did not attain an urban majority until 1920; before then most Americans were rural or lived in small towns. This demographic shift to the city continued, but many urban dwellers were there reluctantly, displaced from their rural homes in search of jobs. Presidential candidate Al Smith discovered in 1928 that a statistically urban America would still not elect an urban candidate for president. His immigrant parents, Roman Catholicism, New York accent, and urban predilections were unacceptable to many rural Americans and urban dwellers with strong rural roots. Franklin Roosevelt learned from Smith's experience and during his successful presidential campaigns of 1932 and 1936 emphasized his early gentry farmer days in Dutchess County rather than his more recent residences in Albany and New York. By the time Willkie entered politics in 1940, the Great Depression had intensified a nostalgic view of rural America as a better place than cold city sidewalks filled with breadlines for the unemployed.

Indiana had also attained an urban majority in 1920, but it had more difficulty accepting this new reality than did most other states. Many Hoosiers clung tenaciously to their memories of a rural past. The Indianapolis 500 race might symbolize the state's technological future, but that was for only one weekend in a year. The authentic Indiana was represented at the State Fair, which was the culmination of ninety-two county fairs where the produce of Hoosier soil was paraded, tasted, weighed, and awarded prizes for days on end. Regardless of the rising skyscrapers in Indianapolis and Fort Wayne, the highest point in most Hoosier towns was the church steeple or the grain elevator, just as it had always been. Lake County, with its steel mills and burgeoning population of recent immigrants from Eastern Europe, could not be entirely ignored, but it could be classified as aberrant—the Region—and unlike the real Indiana. Hoosier author Theodore Dreiser accepted the new reality of urban life and was therefore rejected by many Indiana readers and critics. Wealth and national fame might come to this chronicler of harsh urban scenarios, but not popularity and acceptance in his home state; that was reserved for Riley and Tarkington. If Wendell Willkie wanted to disassociate himself from urban stereotypes in 1940 and resurrect a rural Hoosier past for political gain, he needed merely to walk backward down the dusty path into the nineteenth century that his home state had so doggedly kept alive. Hoosiers seemed to prefer this anachronism, and Willkie found it tailored to his needs.

Of the many qualities that characterized Willkie's behavior, independence was one of the most distinctive. He marched to his own drumbeat, acting on personal principle even when that course was controversial or potentially damaging. His dramatic jump from a lifetime membership in the Democratic party into the arms of the Republicans in 1940 was the most memorable of several such unpredictable actions. This streak of stubborn individualism was decidedly Hoosier in character, and many writers of Indiana history have commented on its pervasiveness. Independent thought can be seen especially in the Hoosier propensity to espouse unusual or unpopular causes, and in the frequent display of political fickleness or capacity for switching political allegiance.

Many noteworthy Hoosier politicians had displayed this independent streak long before Willkie. In the mid–nineteenth century Congressman George W. Julian established a record of political party hopping that would be difficult to match. He started his political career as a Whig, then moved to the Free Soil party and soon thereafter to the Free Democrats. Because of the Republican party's position on slavery, he next joined the Republicans, abandoned them after the Civil War for the Liberal Republicans, and ended his life of public service back in the Democratic party. Most of these moves, he maintained, came because of changes in the parties, not in his own principles. Senator Jesse Bright, on the other hand, stayed with the Democratic party but was forced out of the U.S. Senate owing to a disagreement over issues. His refusal to condemn slavery, states' rights, and the southern Confederacy cost him his political office and won him the devotion of many southern Indiana Democrats who supported these same, albeit minority, sentiments during the Civil War. In the Progressive era of the early twentieth century, J. Frank Hanly abandoned his Republican party after a term as governor to pursue his most compelling private goal. He ran for the presidency on the Prohibition ticket in 1916.

National party leaders were well aware of Indiana's penchant for voting independently, especially during the half century following the Civil War. So desirable were these unpredictable swing votes in an era when both parties were evenly matched that Hoosier politicians were frequently offered vice-presidential nominations in an attempt to lure Hoosier voters to one or the other party. No state except New York captured the second spot on presidential ballots more often than Indiana. Republicans Schuyler Colfax and Charles W. Fairbanks and Democrats Thomas Hendricks, William English, John W. Kern, and Thomas Marshall all played leading roles in this bidding war for fickle—or independent—voters. The election of 1916 pitted Hoosier vice-presidential candidates Marshall and Fairbanks against each other in a close race that could easily have swung either way.

Willkie's independence came early and naturally. His mother was the first woman in the state to join the legal profession and reportedly the first woman to smoke publicly in Elwood. Her model of individualism was both obvious and dramatic. And from his father Willkie learned to champion unpopular causes. As the attorney for a striking labor union the elder Willkie challenged the corporate establishment of conservative Elwood, and young Wendell assisted him in his fruitless quest to enlist the aid of Clarence Darrow, that famous defender of underdogs. In his high school days Wendell rejected the Methodist church of his parents and joined the local Episcopalian congregation attended by a close friend. He ended his ecumenical journey as a Presbyterian. Willkie's brief flirtation with socialism in college was not so much a case of youthful left-wing radicalism as it was a part of the continuum of his intellectual curiosity and independence. In the 1920s, when millions of Americans and thousands of Hoosiers embraced Ku Klux Klan activities and elected many of its members to government office, Willkie launched a lonely and losing battle against the xenophobic tide. As a delegate to the 1924 Democratic convention he supported a resolution to condemn the Klan, which exerted considerable control over the party. The resolution failed to pass, and Willkie later chided the not-so-independent Democrats for their loss of nerve. He taunted them with a line from one of Riley's poems, "the gobble-uns'll get you ef you don't watch out."

Willkie's most publicized act of independence was to join the Republican party and, within a few months, capture the presidential nomination from lifelong professionals in that organization. As proud as many Hoosiers were to have a native son leading the ticket, this instant switch was too much for some partisans to accept. Former Republican Senator James Watson told Willkie why he opposed his candidacy in a story that soon became legendary both for frequency of repetition and variation in detail. In short, Watson explained that he would not mind if the town prostitute joined his church, but he would have reservations about her leading the choir on her first night of attendance. Following his defeat in November 1940, Willkie remained titular head of the Republican party, but his independent ideas alienated so many Republicans that they denied him renomination in 1944. His growing internationalism offended a party whose major leaders—Robert A. Taft, Arthur Vandenberg, and Thomas E. Dewey—were either isolationists or close to it. Likewise, his growing liberalism and championship of federal social welfare programs violated his party's opposition to these New Deal measures. Willkie had moved so far out of the Republican mainstream by 1944 that it was widely rumored he might return to the Democratic fold, be appointed by President Roosevelt to some government post, or even form an independent organization of his own. That he refused to endorse either party's presidential candidate in 1944 was testimony to an individualism so fierce that it had become politically self-defeating.

Less public than his political independence but equally revealing of his individualism was his defense of unpopular causes at a time when silence would have been more beneficial to his career. His arguments in published articles and in the courtroom spoke of both his personal nobility and his political naiveté. He opened himself to charges of radicalism when he argued in the *New Republic* (March 18, 1940) that America should be fair enough to extend legal justice to Eugene V. Debs, Sacco and Vanzetti, and Earl Browder despite their advocacy of socialism, anarchism, and communism, respectively. Defending and winning a legal case in 1942 for William Schneiderman, a member of the Communist party, was a dramatic statement by Willkie about freedom of speech. It was politically dangerous at the time, however, even with the Soviet Union as an ally in the war. His article in the *Saturday Evening Post* (June 27, 1942), "The Case for the Minorities," spoke bluntly about the evils of prejudice and the necessity for more tolerance and opportunities for America's ethnic groups. In all these instances, Willkie went beyond what either political party was willing to promise for human rights, and as a result he received considerable criticism for going too far too fast. More to the point, he was too independent for his own good.

It is significant that speeches by Willkie appeared thirty times in *Vital Speeches of the Day,* a bimonthly journal founded in the 1930s to reprint talks and orations which its editors deemed worthy of preserving for future study. That is more than for almost any other person of the time except Roosevelt. It is also significant that only a small number of these speeches related to Willkie's presidential campaign in 1940. They were instead commentaries on social, economic, and international issues of the day. These frequent appearances in the leading publication of oral communication enhanced Willkie's reputation in the field of oratory, a field valued throughout Indiana history and excelled in by many Hoosiers.

During the mid–nineteenth century in Indiana, oratory was as much a necessity as it was an art form, and it continued its vital role into the early twentieth century, when Willkie became a master of it. Public education in the Hoosier state had been sadly lacking, and at times Indiana led all northern states in illiteracy. In lieu of widespread use of the written word, oral expression was the common form of communication. Those who excelled in the art were lionized and drew huge crowds to hear the finer points of oratory. For a widely advertised speech in 1842, Henry Clay, a Kentucky politician and presidential candidate, attracted a crowd to Richmond, Indiana, estimated at twenty thousand, roughly ten times the size of the town. Following the Civil War, Senator Daniel Voorhees from Terre Haute was renowned for his addresses, which extolled the virtues of rural life. One of his colleagues recalled that when Voorhees spoke of Indiana's bucolic charms, he could "hear the whirr of the threshing machine, the whinney of the colt or the tinkle of the cowbells. . . . "[7] Socialist politician Eugene V. Debs, also a Hoosier, polled few Indiana votes but drew large crowds to hear his passionate speeches. Repugnant as his message may have been to many Hoosiers, his orations attracted multitudes. Albert Beveridge developed this same talent while a student at Asbury College (now DePauw University). He practiced expressions and gestures before a fulllength mirror to achieve the desired effects; and later, when he was a lawyer and senator, his speaking skills commanded respect bordering on adulation. Thomas Marshall, as governor of Indiana and later as vice-president, was probably better known as a witty afterdinner speaker than he was as an administrator.

Willkie's family and early education also contributed to his development as an orator. His maternal grandmother, Julia Trisch, was an evangelist who traveled across Indiana on horseback conducting revival meetings with powerful conversion rhetoric. One familiar story of Willkie's youth was the visit in 1900 of William Jennings Bryan to the Willkie home. There America's most famous orator and presidential candidate discussed current events with the family, and by all accounts the young Wendell was smitten with the great speaker's voice and presence. With two attorneys as parents and five siblings as competitors, the Willkie family constituted an ongoing debating society, particularly around the dinner table. Wendell was not naturally athletic, so he gravitated to forensics, using his dinnertable practice to become Elwood's champion high school debater. He continued this activity at Indiana University and was responsible for arranging a guest lecture there by Governor Marshall. During a year of teaching in Kansas his extracurricular activities included sponsorship of the school debating society. Soon thereafter, in tribute to his interest, experience, and ability, his law school classmates selected him class orator in 1916.

Long before Willkie became a political candidate he had established a reputation as an effective and popular speaker. As one of Akron's leading trial lawyers he was in great demand for talks to civic groups. He rarely wrote out his speeches, preferring to speak extemporaneously from a few notes. His large frame, tousled hair, booming voice, and waving arms were a familiar phenomenon, and he appeared to enjoy this intellectual and physical exercise the way other people enjoy hobbies or sports. Willkie's speeches were generally more persuasive than entertaining: direct and simple in prose and frequently interspersed with personal anecdotes and homey metaphors. Many of his speeches in the 1930s attacked federal regulation of business, tax policies, and the Tennessee Valley Authority, and he became one of the most visible and vocal champions of free enterprise in the country. By 1937 he had become so synonymous with this cause that a Works Progress Administration theater production included a character named Wendell Willkie who orated against government intrusions. The following year, in a Town Hall radio debate, Willkie argued that

> for several years the government has taken definite action to show its hostility to business. It must now take definite action to demonstrate the sincerity of its desire to cooperate. . . . The chief reason why government officials and business men fail to understand each other is because one thinks and speaks the language of politics and emotionalism, while the other thinks and speaks the language of economics and realism.[8]

This episode offered a good example of Willkie's practice of symmetrical construction and the art of balancing opposites. It also established Willkie as the New Deal's most notable opponent.

In Willkie's quest for the 1940 Republican nomination and subsequent campaign for the presidency, his oratory was displayed at its best—and worst. His love of spontaneity led him frequently to toss aside prepared texts and speak extemporaneously; this was a crowd-pleasing technique, particularly when he threw the pages of his speech into the air, as he did on several occasions. He could also coin memorable adages that aided his campaign and were much quoted. Typical was the familiar "Only the strong can be free. And only the productive can be strong." It contained a punchy phrase, a memorable message, and a neat symmetry. Willkie's early vow to "roll" his own speeches was admirable but unrealistic. By the end of his candidacy he had delivered more than five hundred speeches, crafted by several writers in many different styles. He was at his best when he was not inhibited by a written text or microphones and could banter with a small group, but those conditions were not always available. The formal acceptance speech before the more than 150,000 people who flooded into Elwood to hear him and the countless stops at railroad stations that followed taxed his physical strength and personal delivery. Medical experts and speech consultants had to harness his energies to prevent him from losing his voice completely. He had to learn, like his early model William Jennings Bryan, that political oratory, while exhilarating, could be exhausting. Throughout the 1940 campaign he left a lasting impression on thousands who came to hear him; there was passion and principle combined in an old-fashioned stump speech. Wearing his usual rumpled suit, his hair falling over his eyes and arms flailing, Willkie would warn that if Roosevelt were elected for a third term democracy would be endangered. He would then emotionally exhort the crowd to "help me, help me, help me" save it. Grandmother Trisch from her nineteenth-century revival circuit would have recognized his technique and been pleased.

The Willkie speech most frequently mentioned as his finest is the one heard by the largest audience, the one that represented his most mature thinking. Upon his return from a world tour in 1942, Willkie delivered a thirty-minute talk over the four available radio networks to an audience estimated at thirty-six million. He worked on the speech in Rushville while he recuperated from the forty-nine-day trip, which covered thirty-one thousand miles. It was a report on the state of the war, his impressions of foreign opinion about the United States, and his hopes for the postwar world. The speech was intimate in that it frequently used the first-person pronoun and compared distant sites with similar ones in the United States and Indiana in particular. He crafted the talk for aural comprehension with short sentences, rhetorical questions followed by simple answers, repetition of concepts, and catchy phrases, such as "reservoir of goodwill," which recurred throughout. And the speech was passionate. Willkie spoke of his son in the navy and of his hope that following the war the world would be a better place for everyone's children. "Other peoples, not yet fighting," he explained, "are waiting no less eagerly for us to accept the most challenging opportunity of all history—the chance to help create a new society in which men and women the globe around can live and grow invigorated by freedom."[9] The immediate, positive, and powerful response to this speech convinced Willkie that America had grown, along with him, beyond provincial borders and local concerns. Hoosier oratorical roots had produced a speaker with worldwide visions.

The memorial at Wendell Willkie's gravesite in Rushville is a monument to a writer. Just below a granite cross is a huge book carved from stone, its open pages filled with words written by the man now beneath Hoosier soil. Two things are remarkable about this tribute to a literary man. One is that so many other aspects of his career could have been commemorated; the other is that the tribute places him in an impressive line of Hoosier writers of his generation. He had been very successful as a lawyer, businessman, and public speaker, and his political career was galvanic, if not ultimately successful. These parts of his public life are important and well known to many Americans. That his memorial should overlook these aspects and focus instead on his literary pursuits would have pleased Willkie immensely, for it associated him with Hoosiers whom he revered and who had made Indiana distinctive. Willkie the author left a legacy of publications whose ideas and shelf life transcend his legal, business, and political contributions.

While it may have seemed unusual for a politician and businessman to harbor literary aspirations, Willkie came from a state that afforded great respect to writers of all backgrounds. He lived during the state's long golden age of literary productivity, when Indiana produced a disproportionate number of popular writers. James Whitcomb Riley's verses glorified the rural good life, Booth Tarkington's novels analyzed middle-class gentility, Gene Stratton Porter's books for children taught nature and morality, and Ernie Pyle's newspaper columns shared his travels and ruminations. These and dozens more gained fame, wealth, and Pulitzer prizes. One study revealed that between 1900 and 1940 only New York produced more best-selling literary works than did Indiana. A familiar story—possibly apocryphal—describes a traveling lecturer who invited any authors in his Indiana audience to stand and be recognized. To the speaker's surprise, all but one person stood. To his further surprise, he was informed that the one still seated was also an author but was deaf and had not heard the invitation to stand.

Willkie's appreciation of literature started early and endured. Both of his parents had been schoolteachers before entering law, and his mother had helped to establish the public library in Elwood. Their home was filled with books—some estimates ran as high as seven thousand volumes—stacked in shelves, on floors, in every room and the attic. Willkie's father awakened the children in the mornings by quoting from the classics, and the family read to each other and memorized passages from great authors. This atmosphere continued into Wendell's adulthood. He read about four books a week and preferred a weekend of reading to socializing. His wife recalled the Monday chore of gathering up books strewn about their home, and his son remembered being read to as a child from a variety of works. As a politician on the campaign trail in 1940 and 1944, Willkie packed his luggage with books for information and relaxation. Once in Nebraska, a friend recalled, none of his books was handy and the candidate began reading from the local telephone directory. Journalist Roscoe Drummond visited Willkie in his hospital room shortly before his death and noted that a dozen or so recently published books were within arm's reach of his bed.

Willkie's friendships reveal the importance he attached to the literary life. To understand why writers rather than his colleagues in law and business became his closest friends, one need only listen to his own explanation: that he found writers intellectually lively. Some of his chief political advisers were not politicians at all; they were writers, mainly journalists with whom he felt a kindred bond. Russell Davenport from *Fortune,* Joseph Barnes from the *New York Herald Tribune,* and the Cowles brothers, Gardner and John, both publishers, all occupied spots within his inner circle. During his presidential campaign in 1940, some two hundred writers endorsed his candidacy in a fullpage newspaper advertisement, unusual for that time. Included were Hoosiers Booth Tarkington, George Ade, and John T. McCutcheon. Perhaps his closest friend for many years was Irita Van Doren, an editor at the *Herald Tribune*. She hosted many dinners and parties that helped introduce Willkie to other people in the literary world. Of the many events he attended and the many people he met during a trip to England in 1941—government leaders, military officers, laborers, and farmers—he seemed to derive the most pleasure from a special dinner party of English authors arranged by Van Doren. And of all his speeches and remarks quoted in the press during this brief visit with the British, the most memorable involved literature. When he toured the bombed and burned-out area near London's St. Paul's Cathedral and learned of the destruction of many book publishing firms with their millions of volumes, he observed, "They have destroyed the place where the truth is told."[10]

As an author, Willkie took the craft of writing seriously. His prose was expository, not fictional or poetic, and it was designed to inform, not entertain. "I pretend to no literary skill," he insisted; "I write what I think and then rewrite."[11] Barnes believed that Willkie appreciated good writing and possessed the discipline needed to accomplish it. He remembered Willkie pacing the floor, talking out his ideas, rewording until he achieved the right effect. Other people might assist him with organizational ideas, but no one was a ghostwriter for him. Willkie would sit with a manuscript, sucking the end of a pencil and making changes in the copy until he was satisfied. His editorial revisions continued with the printer's proof sheets, and he would sometimes place several telephone calls in a day to his publisher to make last-minute changes.[12]

Much of Willkie's writing was similar to his oratory in that it was intended to convert others to his causes, whether they were economic, political, or international. He had a crusading zeal to share his ideas and experience, so his publications were, at the same time, personal and evangelical. Reviewed chronologically, Willkie's articles in popular periodicals document a writer who was growing in the breadth of his interests and the depth of his understanding. Most of the articles in the mid to late 1930s were an extension of his oratorical opposition to New Deal policies and his defense of free enterprise. "Campaign against the Companies" (*Current History,* May 1935) and "Horse Power and Horse Sense" (*Review of Reviews,* August 1936) both advocated less regulation of business. "Brace Up America" (*Atlantic Monthly,* June 1939) and "Idle Money, Idle Men" (*Saturday Evening Post,* June 17, 1939) both attacked federal tax and spending policies. Interestingly, these two articles are essentially one piece, the former written in a slightly more sophisticated style and the latter in a more homey idiom. In 1940 much of Willkie's writing was political to further his quest for the White House. "The Court Is Now His" (*Saturday Evening Post,* March 9, 1940) attacked the growing power of the chief executive, and "We the People" (*Fortune,* April 1940) set forth his personal goals for the Republican party. Following his loss in the election, Willkie's foreign travels brought a new international focus to his writing. "Give Your Children a World Outlook" (*Parents,* November 1942) and "We Must Work with Russia" (*New York Times Magazine,* January 17, 1943) previewed the publication of *One World.*

Having failed to gain renomination by the Republican party in 1944, Willkie wrote a series of articles that were printed in several newspapers, then published as a pamphlet, *An American Program,* the week of his death. The style was his same simple, direct prose with many personal references, but the substance had grown beyond his earlier work. His interests had become complex and interdependent. Themes of civil rights, internationalism, social welfare, and the benefits of labor unions were interwoven into a larger world view that was no longer Republican or Democratic, conservative or liberal. He hoped this series of articles would force the political parties to reach higher than their current platforms and would also inspire Americans to think beyond old traditions and selfish goals. *An American Program* also departed from contemporary public opinion; these ideas were ahead of their time in 1944. Willkie was exhibiting his strong independent streak, in the tradition of Julian, Bright, and Debs. His evangelical prose might be momentarily unpopular, but its premature message would ultimately prevail.

Willkie's most sustained piece of writing was *One World,* which resulted from his whirlwind global tour in 1942. Following his radio speech to the nation, Willkie spent several months preparing the book manuscript for publication. He worked in Van Doren's apartment and solicited additional information from friends Gardner Cowles and Joseph Barnes, who had accompanied him on the trip. Appearing in the spring of 1943, *One World* became a publishing phenomenon. It remained on best-seller lists all summer, appeared in condensed versions in many papers and magazines, and was translated and printed in many foreign languages. The book transformed Willkie from a minor literary figure to a major one. "In a life unbelievably full of satisfaction," he admitted, the success of *One World* brought him the "richest satisfaction of all."[13] Barnes agreed and speculated that this was the case because Willkie had now gained respect "in a field he had always revered. . . . "[14]

One World reveals many things about Wendell Willkie the writer. His new international vision is obvious, his Hoosier frame of reference is pervasive, and his literary sensibility suffuses the whole. A large portion of the book is a travelogue by a relatively innocent world traveler. He described natural features, clothing, food, and the war fronts with enthusiasm and a sense of wide-eyed discovery. Frequently his first-person account is made even more personal by comparisons of foreign items with American counterparts. Almost invariably these points of reference are to Hoosier parallels; he pulled comparisons from the Indiana portion of his life, not the Ohio and New York sojourns. For example, a jolting jeep ride over primitive roads in Russia reminded him of stories his father had told him of pioneer Hoosier transportation; a female lawyer from Turkey evoked memories of his path-breaking mother practicing law forty years earlier in Indiana; he compared farms with those in Rushville and wooden boardwalks with similar ones in an earlier Elwood. Amid the inevitable descriptions of war strategy and political and economic conditions and his predictions of future events, Willkie included numerous and detailed discussions of literacy, newspapers, and local libraries, the latter of which he had apparently visited compulsively. The attention and space he devoted to the printed word in foreign lands reflected the importance it played in his private world.

Willkie's prose in *One World* was the same as in his earlier publications, straightforward and businesslike. On rare occasion he indulged in mild humor or rose to eloquence. Miles from the comforts of his Manhattan apartment, he discovered "technological backwardness along with poverty and squalor. Any American who makes this comment lays himself open, I realize, to the charges of being overconscious of bathtubs."[15] In his attempt to allay traditional American fears of godless communists, Willkie insisted that "Russia is neither going to eat us nor seduce us."[16] And in his final chapters, which advocate more international cooperation, he recalled that "I was a soldier in the last war and after the war was over, I saw our bright dreams disappear. . . . " Then he urged readers not to allow that to happen again.[17]

His untimely death at age fifty-two left many of Willkie's dreams unfulfilled. A surprising number of them were literary. On several occasions he had spoken of plans to write books about the Civil War, American dynasties, and civil rights. On other occasions he had discussed the possible purchase of such newspapers as the *Chicago Daily News* and the *Indianapolis Star.* He had speculated about leaving law and business and retiring to Rushville to write full time. None of these plans bore fruit, however. His literary life was brilliant yet brief, like the flambeaux of natural gas that lit the night skies of his native Elwood. Optimistic and illuminating, they both expired before fulfillment. Regardless of its brevity, Willkie's writing career was significant. He planted words, a commodity as valuable in Indiana in his day as corn and soybeans. And the harvest of his literary labor was less perishable than the fragile rural image, independence, and oratory which he and other Hoosiers cultivated in such abundance.

NOTES

1. *New Republic,* August 23, 1943, 241.
2. *Time,* July 31, 1939, 42.
3. *Newsweek,* August 19, 1940, 16.

4. *New Yorker,* October 19, 1940, 23.

5. John Bartlow Martin, *Indiana: An Interpretation* (New York, 1947), 10–11.

6. *Indianapolis Star,* May 16, 1940, and Joseph Barnes, *Willkie* (New York, 1952), 11.

7. Leonard Kenworthy, *The Tall Sycamore of the Wabash* (Boston, 1936), 45.

8. Wendell L. Willkie, *This Is Wendell Willkie* (New York, 1940), 70–71.

9. *Vital Speeches,* November 1, 1942, 39.

10. *London Times,* January 28, 1941.

11. Barnes, *Willkie,* 313.

12. Ibid., 313–14.

13. *New York Times,* May 7, 1943.

14. Barnes, *Willkie,* 316.

15. Wendell L. Willkie, *One World* (New York, 1943) 19.

16. Ibid., 86.

17. Ibid., 171.

MARK H. LEFF

Strange Bedfellows

THE UTILITY MAGNATE AS
POLITICIAN

WHEN DEMOCRATIC business tycoon turned Republican nominee Wendell Willkie gave Franklin Roosevelt his toughest battle for the presidency, he brought with him a background that would have withered the political prospects of lesser men. Even his personal life posed vulnerabilities; his ongoing relationship with literary editor Irita Van Doren was an open secret among reporters, one that President Roosevelt might not have been above exploiting had the going gotten rougher. But as the band played "Let Me Call You Sweetheart," Edith Willkie dutifully joined her husband on the campaign trail. "Politics," she is said to have remarked, "makes strange bedfellows."[1]

No stranger, at least in retrospect, than the shotgun marriage of Wendell Willkie and the Republican party. Forsaken first by the electorate in 1940, then more definitively by his own adopted party in 1944, Wendell Willkie become a historical *disparu* for both parties, neither of which came to terms with the fact that a so-called genuine liberal[2] could become the Republican standard-bearer. And even on the hundredth anniversary of Willkie's birth, what we tend to remember, and what many are inclined to celebrate—his "One World" internationalism, his progressive positions on race and civil liberties, his positive response to Roosevelt's feelers about forming a new "liberal" party—offers precious little guidance in understanding Willkie's political rise, and in particular the ways in which his business activities underwrote his political emergence.

While it is true that Willkie ended his career by denouncing "free enterprise" propaganda from certain "powerful groups who have not practiced real enterprise in a generation" and by upbraiding an audience of Republican politicos and businessmen as "a bunch of political liabilities, anyway," his positions had not always been so heretical.[3] After all, Willkie first established his reputation not as a modern liberal but as the utility executive who took on the New Deal. Willkie rose to prominence not just as a defender of business but of big business, and not just of big business but of one of the nation's most discredited forms of monopoly power, a public utility holding company. There must be more to this utility magnate turned politician, and to the political context from which he emerged, than commonly meets the historian's eye.

Historians make their living, such as it is, by explanations. And if Wendell Willkie had continued to spend his life in relative public obscurity, as a kind of winning loser, a capable but ultimately unsuccessful business counterpuncher, explaining his failure to break into politics would have been child's play. In the only somewhat exaggerated reaction of one Republican national committeeman in 1939, "So I am supposed to go back to the clubhouse and tell the boys that we will all have to pull together now to get the nomination for Wendell Willkie. They'll ask me 'Willkie, who's Willkie?' And I'll tell them he's the President of the Commonwealth & Southern. The next question will be, 'Where does that railroad go to?' And I will explain that it isn't a railroad, it's a public utility holding company. Then they will look at me sadly and say, 'Ken, we always have thought you were a little erratic, but now we know you are just plain crazy.' And that would be without my even getting to mention that he's a Democrat."[4]

This committeeman in fact became a Willkie booster. But on its face his analysis makes political sense. Willkie *was* a relative unknown; though his name—or the misspelled single-l version of it—

surfaced frequently enough in news stories or in political and business journals, it would have been better fare for news trivialists than for everyday political discussion.[5] Willkie *was* a lifelong, self-described "ardent Democrat." He had been a delegate to the 1924 Democratic convention and a contributor to Roosevelt's campaign in 1932 (though in 1936 he voted for Landon); not until 1939 did he shift his registration to Republican, and even then he was still explaining that "the reason I voted Republican in '36 was because I thought those in charge of the Democratic Party were no longer Democratic" (or, as he later more succinctly put it in a preview of Ronald Reagan: "I did not leave my party. My party left me"). He had even cultivated a loose but later politically embarrassing association with the ultimate symbol of Democratic party boss politics, Tammany Hall, serving on the New York County Democratic committee, endorsing the reelection of the notoriously corrupt mayor Jimmy Walker, and complaining about the "very unfair attacks" upon "the organization." Not surprisingly, then, a leading die-hard Republican from Willkie's home state was less than supportive of his presidential aspirations, drawling, "Well, Wendell, you know that back home in Indiana it's all right if the town whore joins the church, but they don't let her lead the choir the first night." When Willkie's acceptance speech to the Republican convention included the ill-considered phrase "And so, you Republicans, I call upon you to join me," a sensitive Republican Old Guard would indeed shake their heads, never providing him with unrestrained support.[6]

There was worse political poison to come. Willkie's rise to the top of the corporate world coincided almost precisely with a Great Depression that—in the words of Walter Lippmann—brought business leaders down "from one of the highest positions of influence and power that they have ever occupied in our history to one of the lowest." In 1929, after a sparkling career as a young corporate lawyer in Akron, Willkie moved to New York to become the chief lawyer for a newly formed public utility holding company, the Commonwealth and Southern Corporation (C&S). By 1933, still only forty years old, Willkie had been jumped over fifty junior executives to become the president of that holding company, and for the rest of the decade he would be its spokesman and chief executive officer.

With his upper Fifth Avenue apartment, his $75,000 salary, and an office one block off Wall Street, he had made it, even if this exalted position threatened to neutralize whatever public relations mileage he might otherwise derive from his small-town Indiana origins (Harold Ickes, for example, would ridicule him in the 1940 campaign as a "simple barefoot Wall Street lawyer").[7]

But this was not an easy time to be prime defender of public utilities. Within weeks of Willkie's arrival in New York, the stock market crashed, ultimately sending C&S stock down to 1 5/8 from its high of 23 3/4. Worse still was the political fall-out from the holding companies that had simply shattered. Newspapers overflowed with indignant denunciations of bankrupt utility empires such as disgraced multimillionaire Samuel Insull's.

The mechanism for controlling sprawling networks of electric companies with relatively small investments was so complex that even some of the manipulators themselves could lose track. The basic idea was to strictly limit the percentage of each electric company's capital that carried voting rights, so that a relatively small investment could secure the voting rights to control that company. An "intermediate holding company" would then purchase a controlling share of that voting stock. Through an identical maneuver, another holding company could then control both the intermediate holding company and all of its operating subsidiaries by obtaining a controlling share of *its* limited voting stock, continuing on up a pyramid capped by a small group of investors. This leveraged position allowed these investors to use their cheaply purchased voting rights to control a network of electric companies—siphoning off their profits, perhaps, by forcing them to pay inflated prices for financial services and supplies provided by the investor group.

When these precarious empires collapsed in spectacular fashion, hundreds of thousands of investors and consumers alike concluded that they had been bilked and that their state utility regulators had been bamboozled. Reckless and unethical utility promoters had manipulated the securities of power companies, and those utilities in turn were able to overcharge by artificially inflating their rate base and shamelessly influencing local legislators, educators, and newspapers.

Power companies thus became a prime symbol of the excesses of the 1920s. They had precious few defenders. Even traditional American antigovernment attitudes offered little protection to utilities; the essential services they provided, the monopoly positions they were accorded (duplicate electric lines made no sense, especially given the huge investments a power grid required), and the special relationships with government they cultivated (such as the power of eminent domain, and sometimes the use of governmentally controlled water power) all lent them a public character that distinguished them from other businesses and seemed to necessitate careful regulation.

With so many detractors and so few defenders, public utilities thus provided an easy mark for politicians. Perhaps the best indicator of that is the fact that Franklin Roosevelt singled the industry out for exceptional penalties—both competition from the Tennessee Valley Authority (TVA) and the prospect of mandatory restructuring under the Public Utility Holding Company Act of 1935. As historian Ellis Hawley has shown, political vulnerability, not potential economic impact, was FDR's prime criterion for enemy status. "Judge me," Roosevelt had said in a 1932 campaign speech, "by the enemies I have made. Judge me by the selfish purposes of these utility leaders who have talked of radicalism while they were selling watered stock to the people and using our schools to deceive the coming generation."[8]

One might think that the only thing less propitious for a future political career than being branded an enemy of the people would be to make a spectacle of oneself by leading an open, desperate, and largely futile countercharge. That was the position in which Willkie placed himself. Though well aware of public enmity toward utilities, he threw himself into this political battle with his customary élan, even as some fellow Wall Streeters and utility executives—who trusted more in backstage manipulation than in open political battles and the sorts of strategic concessions favored by Willkie—were labeling him "the Jesus Christ of the utility industry" or urging him to "pipe down for the sake of all of us."[9]

The corporation Willkie headed owned the major utility systems that were to be displaced by the TVA, the regional planning, hydroelectric, and flood control program that rapidly gained renown as one of the New Deal's most ambitious and efficiently administered initiatives. Willkie led the resistance to TVA expansion on every front, driving a very hard bargain in selling C&S's threatened southern affiliates to the TVA, backing suits against the TVA to challenge its constitutionality and to enjoin its expansion, pushing for amendments to TVA in Congress, and using power company money to underwrite sympathetic newspapers and to attempt to defeat municipal referenda for public power.

When Roosevelt proposed the Public Utility Holding Company Act, whose "death sentence" provision originally mandated the abolition of inessential utility holding companies within five years, Willkie spearheaded public opposition to that too. Though Willkie himself was not personally responsible for what became one of the nation's most notorious and underhanded lobbying campaigns, this association could not have improved his reputation. The utilities represented, Congressman Sam Rayburn charged, "the richest and most ruthless lobby Congress has ever known." The Black Committee's sensational investigation of this lavish lobbying effort uncovered evidence of unsavory practices ranging from pressure on employees to send predrafted protests to Congress to one case in which thirteen hundred telegrams against the "death sentence" provision were signed with names copied from the phone book. This power trust, Ellis Hawley points out, "had overreached itself and had become actively hated by a wide variety of people"; it was looked upon as a villain "on a par with Wall Street" for whom "nothing was too bad" (a particularly telling comparison in the case of Willkie, whose associations with Wall Street opened him to charges of being a tool of financial wheeler-dealers, or even being one himself).[10]

At least on the surface the picture thus far does not seem to be a politically promising one. Sporting Wall Street connections, having come to represent what was arguably the most disreputable and "recalcitrant interest group in the country," and positioning himself as an outsider to the party that would nominate him, Wendell Willkie might seem to be an opponent made to Franklin Roosevelt's order.[11]

Yet this picture is misleading, in several critical ways. We know of course that Willkie was no political patsy. He certainly worried Roosevelt's entourage in 1940; even after running a sometimes ill-managed, roller-coaster campaign against a political legend in the shadow of a world war, he still narrowly outpolled Roosevelt outside the South and the nation's largest cities—a result no other Republican would have been likely to better. Besides, Willkie's preexisting reputation at the grass roots was scarcely the determinant of his political rise—not unless one looks, in Alice Roosevelt Longworth's mordant phrase, to "the grass roots of ten thousand country clubs." A campaign that entered the final two months before the convention without a single publicly announced delegate, a campaign launched with appeals to names taken from Yale and Princeton alumni directories, sets off alarm bells when cast as the voice of the people.[12]

Though a remarkable public upsurge did undoubtedly fuel the perception of Willkie as a phenomenon and a "winner," one must also consider his allure to the businessmen who pushed him as one of their own and to the young professionals, advertising executives, business publicists, media moguls, and political operatives who organized on his behalf and powered what one political reporter terms "the greatest publicity bandwagon in the history of American politics." Two thousand Willkie mailing clubs emerged seemingly from nowhere to mail out campaign literature (thanks partly to the generous financial and voluntary support of local power companies). The convention itself was greeted by packed galleries, hundreds of Willkie volunteers (some of them employees of Wall Street firms who had bankrolled their all-expense-paid assistance), and a deluge of hauntingly familiar letters and telegrams (many, reportedly, with phony names and addresses).[13]

Of unmistakable importance in surmounting barriers to political acceptability was the power of Willkie's personality. Contemporary and historical works are unanimous on this point; one, in describing how Willkie "happened" to people, compared it to being struck by a bolt of lightning. His magnetic presence, dynamism, unaffected charm, warmth, enthusiasm, humor, manifest intelligence, common sense, informality (the image of this large man draping his leg over a chair arm seems to have arrested more than one acquaintance), easy command, and winning self-confidence (the same adjectives appear repeatedly) made instant converts, including, importantly, members of the press. Willkie's quickness with a quip, a self-effacing riposte, or a genial needle usually served him well, as when he poker-facedly denied to one political reporter that he and Irita Van Doren were more than "good friends," then kidded him in front of his press colleagues about throwing around charges of having five mistresses. Willkie also could be stirringly persuasive, quotable, and engaging; he lent to themes that listeners had heard dozens of times before a freshness that gained him the somewhat oxymoronic reputation of being the nation's most articulate big businessman. What other businessman would throw off lines like this one from a speech at Indiana University?: "One of the things you will learn in your careers is that the world has a habit of emerging from soul-shattering conflicts with its soul still unshattered." In political exchanges, as in numerous congressional hearings or a triumphant (though, again, apparently packed) radio debate with New Dealer Robert Jackson, his quick thinking, ready wit, and pervasive tone of thoughtfulness and reason won audiences over, and earned him accolades as "about the best man in the country in a knock-down-and-drag-out battle of words."[14]

Perhaps above all, Willkie was a consummate salesman who radiated conviction and sincerity. To an unusual degree he avoided political cant and blatant self-promotion. Admittedly, he played on his country boy Horatio Alger image, parrying an attack with the observation that his boyhood hunting experience in Indiana had taught him that the way to determine which bird was wounded was that "the hit ones always fluttered," or allaying his secretary's concerns about his perpetually rumpled suits by pointing out that "it's an asset in my business to look like an Indiana farmer." "I'd watch Willkie," one Republican analyst said in 1939. "He still has his haircuts country style." Yet even as his campaign carefully drew attention to his farm-town roots and his much-beloved Indiana farms, Willkie set limits on the hype. He ceremoniously refused to pose for clichéd campaign photo opportunities in overalls or on a tractor ("I have never done a stroke of work on a Rush County farm in my life, and I hope I never have to," he joked), and disarmingly pronounced in his nomination speech that "I am a businessman . . . formerly connected with a large company"—"a connection of which I am very proud."[15]

Finally, Willkie profited from a reputation as a down-home intellectual; he was a voracious reader with wide-ranging knowledge and a facile intelligence, all of which he profitably displayed as a guest star in April 1940 on the popular radio quiz show "Information Please." Few politicians or businessmen would have hazarded such a potentially humiliating experience; one shudders to think of the results if a current youthful fair-haired political son of Indiana placed himself in such a position. In fact, as *Life* rather cruelly pointed out, until Willkie, "no big businessman had ever been asked to participate—presumably because no businessman could be found with adequate funds of scholarship and wit." Yet Willkie "proceeded to hold his own with the experts in an impressive and altogether engaging fashion." This was no ordinary politician.[16]

That distinctiveness was itself a key to Willkie's rise, just as it would prove to be a contributor to his marginality in Republican circles at the end of his career. Especially to a party with a tired, losing image as the party of Depression there were decided advantages to going outside the political arena to select a candidate who seemed above traditional partisan bickering. Though this quest for a fresh face has customarily led besieged out-parties to resort to military men rather than businessmen, Willkie otherwise fit the bill. Despite gratifying gains in the 1938 congressional elections, many Republicans knew they needed the kind of help that their flawed collection of presidential aspirants in 1940 might not be able to provide. In their desperation to return from political exile, Republicans proved willing to bend the political rules. Candidate Robert Taft's wife Martha was on the mark in her assessment that Willkie's nomination could not have happened "if the party hadn't been jittery." Willkie's various departures from politics as usual made him very much an unknown quantity, but there are times when looking like a winner can be recommendation enough.[17]

Besides, a political outsider position—the very absence of a political record—can be a distinct asset in a time of sweeping change. Willkie's business concerns had focused entirely on domestic issues; while most Republican leaders assumed proneutrality positions in the 1930s, he had been almost silent. Thus in the crisis atmosphere of the spring and summer of 1940, with the terrifying success of the Nazi blitzkrieg across Europe, Willkie was freer than most to distinguish himself from his Republican opponents by taking a vigorous position in favor of aid to the Allies. This internationalist position proved especially important in attracting key elite Eastern support to Willkie, and its broader public appeal—combined with the fact that Willkie's easy sense of command made him a more credible crisis leader than, say, the callow Tom Dewey—is recognized as "decisive" in securing Willkie's nomination.[18]

Yet to explain Willkie's nomination in terms of his internationalism, his nonpolitical status, and his personal skills would be to ignore the central role of his business career in his "miraculous" political ascent. The nature of that role is not obvious. Unlike the appeal of that other business leader turned nominee, Herbert Hoover, Willkie's appeal was not based on supposed extraordinary managerial skills. Willkie, unlike Hoover, could not lay claim to a bold new economic vision that only he could administer. Even the most prominent parallel, that neither had ever run for public office (though Hoover, at least, had over a decade of public service behind him), is deceptive. While this picture of disinterested "administrative leadership" free from the corruptions of politics does account for part of Willkie's allure to fellow businessmen,[19] Willkie in fact had never been "outside" or "above" politics. He instead was a master of corporate public relations and the most attractive champion of the mainstream business critique of the New Deal regulatory state. These activities positioned him to take advantage of the political opportunities and vulnerabilities that opened up at the end of the 1930s (a Willkiean Moment, perhaps, for those inclined toward self-parody).

The fundamental reality of Willkie's business career is that his was preeminently, from first to last, a political job. Public utilities by their very nature are dependent on the government that regulates them, and the Democrat Willkie's meteoric rise to the presidency of Commonwealth and Southern was facilitated by his partisan common bond with an incoming administration that had already pledged itself to public power development and the control of holding company abuses. In an industry whose fate rose and fell on its public reputation, power companies had boasted experience in "every conceivable medium of publicity and propaganda . . . except skywriting."[20]

Even on this fastest of corporate public relations tracks, Willkie stood out as the electric industry's most sophisticated salesman and best representative in its battles with the New Deal. He was endlessly soliciting support in letters to stockholders, testifying before Congress, barraging newspapers with press releases and unsolicited letters, meeting with President Roosevelt and his advisers, courting local influentials in his frequent visits to C&S companies (Willkie traveled to every town with a population over two thousand served by his companies), delivering speeches that then might be widely reprinted courtesy of the utilities trade association or his own holding company, and publishing articles for business and utility journals. By 1937 he was even extending his publicity efforts into national radio networks, a "March of Time" movie, and mass-circulation magazines.[21]

With an insight that would later save him considerable grief as presidential candidate, Willkie also recognized that actions of C&S were an essential part of his public relations effort. This connection went beyond the fact that C&S, at least as holding companies go, seemed relatively clean. Even the occasional charges of antilabor practices and political corruption were difficult to pin on Willkie, and he was safe from more telling criticism. He had not sneaked through insider deals to boost his own income, and C&S had refrained from the usual holding company abuses: it had not milked operating companies by vast overcharges for supplies and management services, it had not jacked up utility rates by manipulation of stock values or a topheavy corporate structure, and Willkie had even reduced banker influence on its board of directors. Just as important, the electrical service provided through C&S was influenced by Willkie's management philosophy of public relations. "I sincerely believe," he wrote a local power executive in 1935, "that the way out of all the present mess and criticism of the utilities is to so increase the average domestic use as to very materially lower the average rate." The threat of being pushed aside by cheaper TVA-generated electricity played a role in this higher volume–lower price strategy, especially the grudging campaign to extend power lines to farmers, but C&S price cuts outside the Tennessee Valley indicated that more wide-ranging considerations came into play. One of Willkie's earliest and most important initiatives at C&S was to increase utility usage by slashing rates through an incentive scheme for increased consumer electricity purchases, and by pushing appliance sales through a vastly expanded sales force and liberalized credit terms—with the result that C&S could boast some of the nation's lowest utility rates.[22]

One should not overemphasize these public relations successes. C&S was ultimately dismantled (albeit not until 1949) through the Public Utility Holding Company Act that Willkie had opposed, and C&S's Tennessee Electric Power Company was forced to sell out (albeit at a very respectable price) to the TVA. The southern states where Willkie waged his most intensive public relations battle proved of almost no political value to him if judged by activist support, nomination ballots at the Republican convention, or electoral votes. The TVA itself was arguably even more adept at local publicity, aggressive competitive tactics, and political hardball than the utilities. Given the TVA's lower rates, its image as a savior of the Tennessee Valley, and the debased reputation of the power trust, Willkie's southern campaigns had often achieved little beyond damage control.[23]

Yet even as Willkie was losing the utility battle, his political future was winning a war. Willkie's defense of the utility industry, extended in the later 1930s to a critique of the New Deal itself, was at times couched in a modulated tone of sweet reason that revealed his instinct for public relations. Yet ultimately, and surprisingly given his current reputation, it was less the moderation of his message than his piercing indictment of the regulatory state that positioned him to become the beneficiary of the New Deal's increasing vulnerabilities.

With appropriately chosen quotations, it is not difficult to make a moderate businessman out of Wendell Willkie. In fact, given the conspicuous stridency of business rhetoric at the time, even minimal civility could pass for temperate restraint. As a relative newcomer,

Willkie was in an excellent position to appear fair-minded, concerned about the public welfare, and censorious of past evils of the utility industry and of business as a whole. "A few men have no right to stand in the way of progress—if it is progress," he magnanimously proclaimed. "There is no divine right given to anybody to handle the generation and sale of electrical power." Even his protests against unfair TVA competition with C&S offered the strategic concession that public interests had primacy over private ones. "The only basis upon which the value of the TVA can be judged," he allowed, "is: What is its effect on the country as a whole? In the end, will it help or harm the welfare of the American people?"[24]

Willkie was also quite willing to point to past corporate economic and political "abuses." In glowing terms, he endorsed what he portrayed as the pre–World War I Progressive era's largely successful battle "against domination of the people by Big Business." Especially as his political prospects brightened, Willkie denounced "the money-mad period of the twenties," when "business men, drunk with power," became promoters and "jugglers of finance" in a "system of 1929" that "could not be permitted to stand."[25]

Admittedly, Willkie removed any inconvenient political implications by quickly adding that "the depression overturned this corporate tyranny almost overnight" so that the men with this power were now "without influence." Still, this delicate balancing act could lend Willkie's public pronouncements a persuasive tone of judicious open-mindedness. In opposing utility legislation, for example, he was careful to concede that some holding company regulations were advisable, and in denouncing excessive government interference in free enterprise he disarmingly also criticized businessmen who asked for their own subsidies and protective legislation to insulate them from "normal economic processes."[26]

A number of New Dealers who detested Willkie as a hypocritical smooth operator found this cloak of moderation infuriating. Facing case after nettlesome case brought by the utility industry in its futile attempt to block government competition and further regulation, the National Power Policy Committee's general counsel pointedly chided Willkie that "I have to spend a great deal of time and energy in endeavoring to sustain in the courts provisions to which you and other utility officials publicly state you do not object." The criticism was so close to the mark that Willkie was reduced to an uncharacteristically lame response: "with all of my duties, I no longer get a chance to study in detail the particular form which litigation takes." Willkie's practice of favoring the idea of regulatory or social measures while finding fault with the means for implementing them had a similar manipulatory flavor. "He agreed with Mr. Roosevelt's entire program of social reform and said it was leading to disaster," scoffed Socialist party presidential opponent Norman Thomas.[27]

In fact, what can be just as striking as the overlay of moderation in Willkie's public pronouncements is the undertone of business fundamentalism. This should not be entirely surprising. Passionate advocate that he was, Willkie's "complete identification of himself with the cause in which he was currently engaged" led him to take on much of the political and rhetorical coloration of a corporate environment most notable for its uniformity. This is not to imply that Willkie was a blank slate. Even his tendency to see the world through the prism of the travails of a public utility holding company did not invariably push him in traditional conservative directions. To take the most striking example, his unpleasant experiences with adversarial congressional and executive investigations and actions spurred his inclination to protect First Amendment rights; hence his politically iconoclastic attack upon the Dies Committee's persecution by innuendo, along with other public warnings about government excesses in prosecuting radicals and fascists.[28]

Yet Willkie's basic message on New Deal business policy followed familiar lines. Though he prided himself on writing his own speeches, a remarkable amount of his political rhetoric was pumped from the same shallow reservoir of ideas and language that seems to have supplied most business spokesmen in the mid- and late 1930s. Willkie espoused a trickle-down philosophy that gave top priority to promoting corporate investment. The key was to provide "our industries with venture capital" by offering incentives for wealthier people "who have money to invest"—a position that seemed virtually uninfluenced by the small minority faction among politically active businessmen more concerned with mass consumption and purchasing power. "Huge indiscriminate government expenditures," "a network of Government bureaus and rules," and "excessive" taxes on large incomes and capital gains, he complained again and again, had created a climate of fear that had "scared private investment into hiding," dried up "the sources from which industry gets its capital," and "taken the life out of industrial enterprise." With his own utility industry in particular, the administration's approach had been "brutal, cruel, unfair and un-American."[29]

Willkie thus charged to the defense of big business, whose interests he said extended to smaller firms ("small business and big business prosper under exactly the same conditions, and the conditions that are harmful to one are harmful to the other") as part of a system of "free enterprise which has been responsible for the extraordinarily high level of the American civilization." Seemingly borrowing first from Calvin Coolidge, then, prospectively, from Charles "What's Good for General Motors" Wilson, he first explained that "the United States is a business country, and our government must recognize that in its attitude toward business" and then joined a Chamber of Commerce public relations campaign in proclaiming that "no truer statement was ever made" than "What helps business helps you." At one point, Willkie became so carried away by his own mission and by his equation of free enterprise with patriotism that he declared that "no duty has ever come to me in my life, even that in the service of my country, that has so appealed to my sense of social obligation, patriotism and love of mankind as this, my obligation to say and do what I can for the preservation of public utilities privately owned." It is no wonder that scholars who closely examine Willkie's political stance as business spokesman in the 1930s tend to portray a very different Willkie from the one we now tend to remember, even claiming for him the "virtually unchallenged leadership of conservatism" or arguing that—despite "moderate" touches—he "placed the free enterprise ideal before the American people" in a way that furthered business "fundamentalist" themes.[30]

If such statements were all there were to Wendell Willkie's philosophy, one might be skeptical of his appeal to Americans, who had heard it many times before. One somewhat misleading clue to why that skepticism would be misplaced lies in the fact that Willkie so persistently and unapologetically—in his correspondence, conversation, and speeches—made a point of calling himself a liberal. In these days of the "l-word," that self-designation not only paints a deceptive picture of Willkie's politics; it seems to verge on masochism. Yet it must be remembered that in the 1930s liberalism had an allure that made it a standard very much worth capturing; even Herbert Hoover and the American Liberty League had desperately fought to retrieve it from the New Deal and return it to its foundation in classical liberalism and Jeffersonian principles of freedom from governmental restraints. It seemed, as Willkie himself admitted with pardonable exaggeration, that "these are days when every man calls himself a liberal."[31]

The definition of liberalism did not long remain contested terrain. Franklin Roosevelt helped to close off this debate in definitively associating liberalism with activist government, diminished autonomy for corporate leadership in relations with labor and the public, and what historian David Green has pejoratively portrayed as a coercive "politics of governmental generosity."[32] The temptation is thus all the greater to see Willkie's rearguard claim to liberalism as round-about evidence of what we now call conservatism. Labels are indeed confusing—and thus peculiarly unrevealing—in Willkie's case, especially with the shifting emphasis of his own political message in the post-1940 period, when his involvements in the broader political arena freed him from the constraints, obligations, and reigning perspectives of his former corporate environment.

Despite occasional lapses, Willkie was never so immersed in the business world that he lost his instinct for public relations and his sensitivity to what sold and what grated, to what seemed sanctimonious or phony. He did not join other industrialists in vilifying Franklin Roosevelt or labor unions, and he avoided the transparently self-serving claims of "public service" that others used in making a case for the utility industry. Willkie's defenses of his own liberalism, as predictable as they were in some aspects, also offer critical insights into his political appeal. At times he defined liberalism in terms of the "moderate middle of the road course" that he liked to claim as his own. A liberal, he explained in a speech at Indiana University, seeks "to strike a true balance between the rights of the individual and the needs of society."[33]

Willkie thus boasted of "a new and far more enlightened attitude toward their social responsibilities" among business executives and endorsed at least "most of the objects" of a wide range of popular New Deal reforms. Among the "moral gains of recent years" that he pledged to retain were "the idea of 'truth in securities,' " some provision for " 'social security' for the aged and the unemployed," "provisions for collective bargaining," and "the principle of federal supervision over industrial activities." To be sure, these expressions of support for recent "vast new obligations" were generally couched so vaguely as to allow anything short of outright repeal, and Willkie in fact proceeded to suggest revisions aplenty. But the tone itself was important. When Willkie's campaign for nomination and election led him to offer a more venturesome, specific set of endorsements—an expanded government public welfare role to include responsibility for the destitute and "elementary guarantees of public health," crop insurance, soil conservation, more ambitious slum clearance, opposition to "business monopolies," minimum wage and maximum hour standards, civil rights, even rural electrification and the continuance of other power projects—Willkie admittedly disturbed some of his supporters (one turned to his wife during Willkie's acceptance speech and muttered, "Where in hell did he get this?"), but his earlier portrayal of his own liberalism and moderation had laid the groundwork to make this me-tooism seem something less than a volte-face.[34]

But most important, Willkie's conception of liberalism penetrated to areas in which the New Deal seemed increasingly vulnerable. Central to his philosophy as business spokesman was a call to arms against the encroachments of "Big Government"—a theme that stood out ever more sharply against the backdrop of the advancing menace of fascism. In his own mind and in the image he projected, liberalism linked his persisting admiration for Woodrow Wilson progressivism to his opposition to New Dealism. The abuse of concentrated monopoly power was a worthy villain, he argued, one that merited the assault against "corporate domination" by "the liberal movement of the first fifteen years of this century." But now this enemy of liberalism had "changed its shape—it now wears the guise of government." The result of the New Deal, he warned, "was not to eliminate monopolistic control, but *merely to change its ownership*" in the form of "political monopoly." "In the pre-war years we fought against domination of the people by Big Business. We now face the domination of the people by Big Government." The parallels that Willkie drew were quite systematic:

> Too much power in the hands of a few men; use of money to influence political decisions; manipulation of the markets; destruction of all op-position—these were the charges hurled against the economic mon-opolies of the first quarter of this century. They are the charges which we make today against the present form of government. The banners used by the true liberals today are the same banners used by the liberals in that other time.[35]

The themes presented here, including the wail of old progressives that their crusade against concentrated power had been betrayed, were already familiar to Depression-era audiences, though Willkie presented them more compellingly and thoughtfully than most. But when Willkie hammered this critique home with frequent references to Hitler, Mussolini, and Stalin, when he claimed a special urgency from the fact that "liberalism has lost in perhaps half of the territory of the world," and when he pointed to an ominous worldwide trend toward dictatorial government, he revealed an instinct for the vul-nerability of New Deal reform in the intensifying world crisis.[36]

As a utility spokesman, Willkie was fortuitously well located to exploit these themes. The dangers of a permanent regulatory state and of abused government power had been a rhetorical staple for him in his battle against the TVA. Even when Willkie moved to voicing a more wide-ranging critique of the New Deal, he carefully cast himself in the role of the star victim of New Dealism run ramp-ant. "I can assure you it is not pleasant," he warned, to have "your reputation smeared with the mud of false insinuation" and your business undermined by a federal "invasion" of unfair competition, business-hating bureaucrats, and punitive regulations. Central to Willkie's pitch in speeches to businessmen was the contention that "the government's attitude toward the utilities will be ultimately the measure of its attitude toward all American enterprise." Even the "drive for government ownership of utilities," he said, was just a first step; "the appetite for victims will grow strong again." "It's my baby that's hurt now—maybe it will be your baby later," Willkie told one business audience.[37]

As Willkie himself confidently recognized, his appeals to the always rich vein of American antistatism, and in particular to deep-rooted suspicions of arrogant bureaucrats and a hostile regimenting state, resounded with increasing effectiveness in the late 1930s, especially when allied with his promise to return to a more productive America under "a businesslike administration" that would unleash the dynamism of free enterprise. Historians today are coming to recognize the late 1930s as one of the last gasps of a bold political vision of "capable administrators who would seize command of state institutions, invigorate them, expand their powers when necessary, and make them permanent forces" in regulating the inevitable conflicts of the marketplace. Willkie's favorite target—heavy-handed regulation by capricious government commissions that "fail to realize that, while a strait-jacket will keep a man out of trouble, it is not a suitable garment in which to work"—seemed particularly well-chosen to counter this particular New Deal vision of an active regulatory state to reshape the economy.[38]

In the early 1940s, Willkie increasingly supplemented this economic critique with other concerns, embracing racial equality, civil liberties, and an internationalist vision of something that could be interpreted as a world New Deal. This ideology arguably set the stage for many postwar "liberals" who would subordinate structural economic change and redistribution of income to government promotion of capitalist economic growth and "safety net" security. But in the context of the late 1930s, Willkie's emphasis on New Deal overregulation drew its significance more from the ways that it paralleled the conventional business case against the New Deal. That case seemed to be validated by the cataclysmic "Franklin D. Roosevelt recession" of 1937–1938. Half the economic gains of the New Deal years vanished in a matter of months, cutting the ground out from under New Deal claims of economic competence. Business leaders used this opportunity, sometimes in ambitious public relations campaigns, to ratchet up efforts to sell themselves and their critique of the New Deal, which helps explain their attraction to Willkie, who was becoming known as the best salesman that they had to offer. With the discrediting of New Deal economic policies, many in the public and Congress seemed inclined to listen. One business editor confessed himself "more encouraged over the evolution in the public attitude than discouraged over the contraction in trade and industry." For all the loyalties that many of its programs had built up, the New Deal was becoming something to be reined in, modified, not expanded upon. The political initiative had shifted, as Roosevelt himself recognized in a much-heralded "business appeasement" campaign in early 1939. It didn't work. Most respondents in public opinion polls deemed the Roosevelt administration "not friendly enough" to "big business," and believed that this attitude had hindered recovery. Asked to choose between the ideas and leadership of the administration or big businessmen as a way of improving the economy, more Americans came down on the side of big business.[39]

Though these beliefs did not translate into a demand for a businessman as president (Willkie was the only corporate head seriously considered as a presidential possibility), they made it possible for a businessman with Willkie's appeal to emerge from the pack and to appear as a possible winner. This was all the more true because Roosevelt's "bubble of invincibility" had burst by 1938—a vulnerability that went well beyond the recession.[40] Roosevelt's abortive proposals in 1937 to "pack" the Supreme Court, to establish seven TVA-like regional planning authorities, and to restructure the executive branch of government only succeeded in simultaneously bringing home inchoate fears of a presidentially dominated all-powerful state at home and the specter of rising dictatorship abroad.

The 1938 elections reflected this change in mood. Republicans still were unmistakably a minority party, but their rise from the ashes of the Democrats' 1936 landslide was dramatic: a net gain of eighty-one seats in the House (not a single Republican incumbent had lost), eight more in the Senate, plus thirteen governorships. Significantly, while the most liberal Democrats found their ranks decimated, Republicans received an object lesson in political strategy from the electoral success of a much-expanded group of eastern Republicans who had made their peace with the more popular New Deal reforms (public opinion polls in fact showed substantial majorities recommending that the Republican party should become more liberal and the Roosevelt administration more conservative).[41]

Other underlying public attitudes also set the stage for a Willkie candidacy. Louis Galambos's study of the changing public image of big business indicates that by the end of the 1930s animosity toward giant corporations had dissipated across a broad spectrum of middle-class groups. Not only had the reputation of businessmen revived but, especially significantly for Willkie, the public utilities issue—always too technical in any case to engage the public for an extended period—became less of a potential liability. Unsurprisingly, the public never had a love affair with holding companies, but many feared that talk of abolishing them or turning their subsidiaries over to the government was going too far. Not only did public ownership of utilities seem a less attractive prospect by the end of the 1930s, but the idea of extending the TVA—popular as these projects were in the Tennessee Valley—increasingly encountered opposition, apathy, and doubt. When the public was asked in the summer of 1940 "whether the fact that Mr. Willkie was president of a large utility holding company make[s] you more or less favorable toward him as a candidate for President," 58 percent allowed that it wouldn't make any difference, 20 percent said that it would make them more favorable, and only 14 percent placed themselves in the "less favorable" category.[42]

Thus the times had conspired to provide a political opening for Wendell Willkie. His liabilities, in particular his association with the hated power trust, had lost their force. In an ironic twist, the business-baiting years of the New Deal had provided a crucial platform for Willkie. When things turned sour for the New Deal and business "ideas" gained new luster as the most viable economic alternative, Willkie's role as defender of business, critic of encroaching government, and exponent of "free enterprise" formulas to substitute productivity for New Deal defeatism positioned him for political advance. In the context of the late 1930s, "utility magnate" and "politician" were not incompatible roles.

The ironies continue. Wendell Willkie was persuasive, engaging, charismatic, even awe-inspiring precisely because he did not fit standard business or political molds. A man whose irreverence went so far that he could dismiss errant portrayals of his religious devotion by saying, "I usually sleep on Sundays,"[43] Willkie could be fervent without being stuffy, sanctimonious, or self-righteous. But the critique of the New Deal that launched Willkie's political career was almost stultifyingly orthodox, or might have seemed so had not Willkie's rhetorical skills, magnetic personality, and image of thoughtful moderation made it appear more compelling, penetrating, humane, and commonsensical.

The captivating Willkie, it seems, had been captivated himself. One cannot emerge from a study of Willkie's business career without some suspicion that the uniformities of his business environment, along with his single-minded commitment to the cause, circumscribed his political vision and limited his considerable capacity to recast the political debate. Partly through the influence of Irita Van Doren and her literary circle, Willkie himself came to recognize these bonds. "You can't imagine what limited intellectual interests businessmen have," he confessed.[44] As his associations and horizons broadened and diversified in subsequent years, so did his vision and message.

Yet in the context of American politics Willkie's more limited horizon in the late 1930s was essential to his political emergence. When their paths crossed in 1940, Wendell Willkie and the Republican party were not such strange bedfellows after all. Their mutual attraction was a product of historical timing, as predictable as their later estrangement.

NOTES

1. R. J. C. Butow, "The FDR Tapes," *American Heritage,* February/March 1982, 20–22; Steve Neal, *Dark Horse: A Biography of Wendell Willkie* (Garden City, N.Y., 1984), 144.

2. Ellsworth Barnard, *Wendell Willkie: Fighter for Freedom* (Marquette, Mich., 1966), 3.

3. John Morton Blum, *V Was for Victory: Politics and American Culture during World War II* (San Diego, 1976), 276 and 271.

4. Kenneth Simpson, quoted in Warren Moscow, *Roosevelt and Willkie* (Englewood Cliffs, N.J., 1968), 50.

5. According to one count, Willkie's defenses of the power industry and attacks on the New Deal were covered on more than 150 occasions by the *New York Times* between 1934 and 1939; Fred Rodell, "Wendell Willkie: Man of Words," *Harper's*, March 1944, 308. But even in late 1937 Willkie's name did not crop up in appreciable numbers when respondents to a public opinion poll were asked to name someone in business or industry of whom they approved or disapproved; Hadley Cantril, ed., *Public Opinion: 1935–1946* (Princeton, N.J., 1951), 555.

6. Barnard, *Willkie*, 143 and 166; Willkie to Peter Wynn, August 29, 1939, "Correspondence 1938–1939" folder, "Willkie Correspondence 1929–1944" box, Wendell Willkie Papers, Lilly Library, Indiana University, Bloomington; Willkie to John Sheehy, September 2, 1931, "34. Democratic Organization, New York County (Sheehy, John E.) 1931–1932" folder, Willkie Papers; Willkie to John Sheehy, November 10, 1933, "Democratic Organization, New York County (Sheehy, John E.) 1933–1935" folder, Willkie Papers; James Watson, quoted in Moscow, *Roosevelt and Willkie*, 70; Richard M. Ketchum, *The Borrowed Years, 1938–1941: America on the Way to War* (New York, 1989), 439.

7. Walter Lippmann, "Big Business Men of America," *American Magazine*, April 1934, 18; Neal, *Dark Horse*, 26; Harold L. Ickes, *The Secret Diary of Harold L. Ickes*, vol. 3 (New York, 1954), 396.

8. Ellis W. Hawley, "The New Deal and Business," in John Braeman, Robert H. Bremner, and David Brody, eds., *The New Deal*, vol. 1 (Columbus, Ohio, 1975), 68; Thomas K. McCraw, *TVA and the Power Fight, 1933–1939* (Philadelphia, 1971), 34.

9. Barnard, *Willkie*, 100 and 97.

10. Neal, *Dark Horse*, 32 and 51; Ellis W. Hawley, *The New Deal and the Problem of Monopoly* (Princeton, N.J., 1966), 334 and 342–43.

11. Lee R. Tilman, "The American Business Community and the Death of the New Deal" (Ph.D. dissertation, University of Arizona, 1966), 177.

12. Michael Barone, *Our Country: The Shaping of America from Roosevelt to Reagan* (New York, 1990), 171; Blum, *V Was for Victory*, 265; Neal, *Dark Horse*, 99; Robert S. McElvaine, *The Great Depression: America, 1929–1941* (New York, 1984), 315; Ketchum, *The Borrowed Years*, 418.

13. Moscow, *Roosevelt and Willkie*, 62, 55, and 68; Neal, *Dark Horse*, 105; James T. Patterson, *Mr. Republican: A Biography of Robert A. Taft* (Boston, 1972), 229.

14. Ketchum, *The Borrowed Years*, 413; Neal, *Dark Horse*, 44; Wendell

L. Willkie, *This Is Wendell Willkie* (New York, 1940), 159; Murray Friedman, "Voyage of a Liberal: A Study of the Evolution of Wendell L. Willkie from Conservatism to Liberalism Based on Heretofore Unpublished Sources" (Ph.D. dissertation, Georgetown University, 1958), 110 and 106; Alva Johnston, "The Man Who Talked Back," *Saturday Evening Post*, February 23, 1939, 10.

15. Press Release, September 30, 1937, "1937 Statements and News Releases" folder, "Willkie Speeches Sept. 1930–1937" box (box 1), Willkie Papers; *Fortune*, May 1937, 6, "1937 May *Fortune*" folder, "Willkie Speeches Sept. 1930–1937" box (box 1), Willkie Papers; Herbert S. Parmet and Marie B. Hecht, *Never Again: A President Runs for a Third Term* (New York, 1968), 64; Barnard, *Willkie*, 199.

16. "Wendell Willkie Exhibits Versatility as Guest Star of 'Information Please'," *Life*, April 22, 1940, 80.

17. Hugh Ross, "Was the Nomination of Wendell Willkie a Political Miracle?" *Indiana Magazine of History*, June 1962, 81; Patterson, *Mr. Republican*, 228.

18. Barnard, *Willkie*, 157–58.

19. Robert Burk, *The Corporate State and the Broker State* (Cambridge, Mass., 1990), 274 and 296.

20. Parmet and Hecht, *Never Again*, 59; McCraw, *TVA*, 21.

21. See Barnard, *Willkie*, 125–26 and 98–101.

22. Johnston, "The Man Who Talked Back," 34; Barnard, *Willkie*, 94–95 and 528; Willkie to Preston Arkwright, December 31, 1935, "Correspondence 1929–1936" folder, "Willkie Correspondence 1929–1944" box, Willkie Papers; McCraw, *TVA*, 74- 77.

23. See McCraw, *TVA*, 146–49.

24. Wendell Willkie, "The TVA Giant and What It Costs to Feed Him," 3 and 8, in "1937, Nov. Chicago Tribune" folder, "Willkie Speeches Sept. 1930–1937" box (box 1), Willkie Papers.

25. Willkie, *This Is Wendell Willkie*, 164–65, 187–88, and 223.

26. Ibid., 188 and 180.

27. Ben Cohen to Willkie, September 8, 1937, and Willkie to Ben Cohen, September 10, 1937, both in "7. Cohen, Ben V. 1937- 1938" folder, "A-O 1921–1940" box, Willkie Papers; Donald Bruce Johnson, *The Republican Party and Wendell Willkie* (Urbana, Ill., 1960), 124.

28. Friedman, *Voyage of a Liberal*, 73; *New York Times*, November 2, 1939, 14; Barnard, *Willkie*, 151–52.

29. Willkie, *This Is Wendell Willkie*, 108, 115, 98–99, 226–27, 241; *Birmingham Age-Herald*, November 24, 1938, "March–Dec. 1938" folder, "Clippings Sept. 1935–March 1939" box, Willkie Papers.

30. Willkie, *This Is Wendell Willkie*, 63; *Jackson Citizen Patriot*, March 1, 1938, and *Salt Lake Tribune*, March 27, 1938, 24, both in "March–Dec. 1938" folder, "Clippings Sept. 1935–March 1939" box, Willkie Papers;

"Radio Talk of Mr. Wendell L. Willkie for 'What Helps Business Helps You Campaign,' " March 9, 1939, in "1939, March 9 Radio What Helps Business Helps You Campaign" folder, "Willkie Speeches Jan., 1938–Dec. 1939" box, Willkie Papers; Willkie, January 1935, quoted in Rodell, "Willkie," 309; Friedman, *Voyage of a Liberal*, 104; Thomas C. Longin, "The Search for Security: American Business Thought in the 1930's" (Ph.D. dissertation, University of Nebraska, 1970), 300–301.

31. Willkie, *This Is Wendell Willkie*, 218.
32. David E. Green, *Shaping Political Consciousness* (Ithaca, N.Y., 1987), 119–21.
33. *Fortune*, May 1937, 7, "1937 May *Fortune*" folder, "Willkie Speeches Sept. 1930–1937" box (box 1), Willkie Papers; Willkie to Raymond Moley, October 17, 1936, "18. Correspondence, Miscellaneous 1936, Oct.–Dec." folder, Willkie Papers; Willkie, *This Is Wendell Willkie*, 170.
34. Willkie, *This Is Wendell Willkie*, 233, 122, 247, and 149–50; Johnson, *Republican Party and Willkie*, 123 and 138; Friedman, *Voyage of a Liberal*, 232.
35. Willkie, *This Is Wendell Willkie*, 164, 162, 203, 189, 204, 165, and 202.
36. Ibid., 168–69 and 200.
37. *Detroit Free Press*, March 1, 1938, and *Jackson Citizen Patriot*, March 1, 1938, both in "March–Dec. 1938" folder, "Clippings Sept. 1935–March 1939" box, Willkie Papers; Wendell Willkie, "New Deal Power Plan Challenged," *New York Times Magazine*, October 31, 1937, 10.
38. Willkie, *This Is Wendell Willkie*, 65 and 104; Friedman, *Voyage of a Liberal*, 132; Philip J. Funigiello, *Toward a National Power Policy: The New Deal and the Electric Utility Industry, 1933–1941* (Pittsburgh, 1973), 267; Alan Brinkley, "The New Deal and the Idea of the State," in Steve Fraser and Gary Gerstle, *The Rise and Fall of the New Deal Order, 1930–1980* (Princeton, N.J., 1989), 92–93.
39. Mark H. Leff, *The Limits of Symbolic Reform: The New Deal and Taxation, 1933–1939* (New York, 1984), 204, 209, and 252; Cantril, *Public Opinion*, 980–81; Tilman, "American Business Community," 51 and 484.
40. Longin, "The Search for Security," 286.
41. Leff, *Limits of Symbolic Reform*, 265; Cantril, *Public Opinion*, 979 and 750.
42. Louis Galambos, *The Public Image of Big Business in America, 1880–1940* (Baltimore, 1975), 229, 237, and 249; Cantril, *Public Opinion*, 481, 694–97, and 1042.
43. Neal, *Dark Horse*, 137.
44. Ibid., 39.

ROSS GREGORY

Seeking the Presidency

WILLKIE AS POLITICIAN

WENDELL WILLKIE ran for one political office in his life: the nation's highest. He served no formal apprenticeship in government or the electoral process. His identity in American history stems, more than any other reason, from the novelty of that quest for the presidency—the excitement of this flash on the national stage, the understanding that here was a story that was not part of the normal course of politics.

And yet, involvement in the swirl of politics was neither inconsistent with Willkie's upbringing and lifelong interests nor out of step with his character and personality. Politics seems to come naturally to lawyers, and so it was with the Willkie family. Wendell earned distinction as an attorney, of course, and both his parents were lawyers. Discussion of current issues regularly pervaded the Willkie household in small-town central Indiana, much of it from Herman Willkie, the father. Herman favored politicians who demonstrated concern for the public good and for the common man, a position he more or less identified with the Democrats. This environment left Wendell—the third son and fourth child (there were six) with an awareness that public issues were matters of normal concern. With equal ease he acquired an attachment to the Democratic party that would last virtually all his life.

Willkie's growth to adulthood sustained the political direction begun in Elwood, Indiana. His arrival at the state university in Bloomington in 1910 came during the Progressive Era, a time when politics gave off a new excitement and new meaning. It would have taken a dull person indeed or one with substantial vested interests to be anything but a progressive in those years, many thought, what with the satisfaction of knowing one was on the side of right and human betterment and, too, the inspiration of following Theodore Roosevelt, Woodrow Wilson, or Robert M. La Follette—the first political heroes since the Civil War.

The vigor of Willkie's reformism at Indiana University placed him on the left side of the progressive movement and even earned him a reputation as an on-campus socialist. In truth Willkie remained a Democrat, a member of the university's Jackson Club. While he claimed to be a follower of Wilson, his endorsement of active government might have placed him closer to Theodore Roosevelt's program of the New Nationalism; and he found much to admire in the courage and humanism of La Follette. Had he decided to take an additional step to socialism he would have regarded it as more the logical evolution of political thought than a radical departure into a new and foreign ideology. There would be much personal meaning in his fondness later in life for the remark that "any man who is not something of a socialist before he is forty has no heart; any man who is still a socialist after he is forty has no head."[1]

Willkie would remain a progressive the rest of his life. He never could forget the potential for evil in concentrated private economic power. Even becoming a big businessman did not lead him to dismiss the notion that business needed supervision. This attitude left him more tolerant than most businessmen of labor unions and of the proposition than an antidote for oppressive capital was government. If he came to question the manner in which public authority was exercised, he could not reject the principle of government as an agent for the public good, acting either as a restraining force or as sponsor of programs for needy social groups.

Moving through the paces of adult life, Willkie kept politics as a major sideline interest and a source of identity. As an attorney in Akron and later in New York, he remained active in the Democratic party, participating in several campaigns and as a delegate to the national conventions of 1924 and 1932. In an age of conservatism, when the Republican philosophy of private management of the economy prevailed, Willkie remained true to his progressive upbringing. A much sought-after speaker, especially in Akron, he lashed out at the Ku Klux Klan and other threats to individual liberties. He retained an admiration for the martyred Wilson and developed warm fondness for the Wilsonian Newton D. Baker. His support for participation in the League of Nations reached almost "religious conviction" at a time when American detachment from political problems abroad stood as virtual holy writ.[2]

Willkie's move to New York and rush up the corporate ladder redefined his relationship to the world of politics in a major way. His remarkable success as corporation attorney and later chief executive officer for the utilities firm Commonwealth and Southern drew him away from participation in lower-level activity and virtually eliminated any prospect—if indeed it existed—of seeking state or congressional office. The long quarrel with the New Deal's Tennessee Valley Authority (TVA) added a new dimension to his political perspective and placed him in position for an astonishing entry into politics at the highest echelon. He lost every part of the battle with TVA but in the end emerged as a virtual winner, extracting a much larger price for his company's property than the government had offered. In speeches, writings, and appearances before congressional committees he established himself as a well-informed, articulate leader of a corporation and a perceptive critic of abuse of power by the administration of Franklin D. Roosevelt. He also introduced himself to influential eastern circles as an attractive individual: outgoing, good-humored, positive, with an engaging personality—the sort of stuff of which political candidates are made.

Presidential politics attracted more than the usual speculation as the United States moved toward the end of the 1930s. Few observers doubted that Roosevelt would obey tradition and retire at the end of his second term, thus creating new opportunities in both parties. The Democrats were expected to choose someone from an uninspiring list of a half dozen or so names, mostly people in Roosevelt's government. Eight years of domination by the Democrats and by Roosevelt had left the Republicans without even a recognizable spokesman. Of the people mentioned as candidates, none showed signs of marching to the front and capturing public attention. A lackluster slate of professional contenders invited the appearance of a newcomer. What would become a movement for Willkie started as an exclusively eastern enterprise of businessmen with heavy representation in New York's publishing world. The only connection to Indiana came from the extent to which the "Willkie appeal" had its foundation in characteristics said to be of Hoosier origin. This was no small consideration, either in explaining why supporters developed such fondness for Willkie or in their interpretation of why he would be an effective candidate. Arthur Krock wrote in the *New York Times* about the appeal of Willkie's rural heritage, and *Fortune's* reference to this "clever bumpkin, the homespun, rail-splitting, cracker-barrel simplifier of national issues" virtually smacked of having found another Lincoln.[3]

Although Willkie brushed aside early mention of his name in politics, his behavior suggested—as his life to that point had indicated—that he was a man of considerable self-confidence and an ambition that recognized few limitations. He began to branch out, make more speeches, write articles on themes that went beyond the problems of Commonwealth and Southern. He scored heavily in a nationally broadcast debate about government and business with Assistant Attorney General Robert Jackson—by most accounts besting this star of the Roosevelt administration, himself said to be presidential timber.

In his expanded activity Willkie found willing assistance from skilled professionals in the publishing business. The extent to which he could charm editors and writers of some of the most prestigious publications was truly remarkable. Irita Van Doren of the *New York Herald Tribune,* who became an exceptionally close friend, helped him polish his writing and in other ways opened doors. The editors of such magazines as the *Saturday Evening Post, Time,* and *Life* added the benefit of their broad circulation base. The prime mover was another editor, Russell Davenport, of *Fortune.* Davenport advised Willkie on ways to publicize his name and helped recruit such influential easterners as Charlton MacVeagh, a publisher with close ties to John D. Hamilton, chairman of the Republican National Committee; Samuel Pryor, a man large in politics in Connecticut; and Kenneth Simpson, national committeeman in New York. In the fall of 1939 Willkie quietly switched registration to the Republican party.

A careful observer might have detected two sides to the political thought of Wendell Willkie at the end of the 1930s. The first, somewhat subdued in recent months but still not abandoned, was of Willkie the liberal, heir of the Progressive Era, possessor of a body of assumptions and reactions that had been strengthened by the jolting experience of the Depression. He had made frequent references to the "money-mad" 1920s and agreed that big business had much to do with the economic collapse. Although his public statements focused on other themes, he had no difficulty supporting the principles and most of the specific programs of Roosevelt's New Deal.

The second Willkie grew out of his recent experience as a corporation executive and his sudden emergence as a long-shot presidential candidate with the Republicans. From this position he was encouraged to see abuses in the recent growth of government activity and find reason for exposing them. The government, after all, had taken over most of his company; and despite several years' effort and expenditure of huge sums of money, Roosevelt's administration had not brought the Depression to an end. Unemployment in 1939 stood at 17 percent. What had started for Willkie as an attack on the specific problem of government competition with private business (the TVA versus Commonwealth and Southern) had expanded by the end of the 1930s into a general assault on the New Deal and political oppression.

Curiously, the two Willkies continued to exist side by side. The new Willkie did not repudiate the old, although the old might be somewhat less conspicuous; he merely added new thoughts to older ones, conflicting though the two might appear to be. The dichotomy perhaps could be explained in Willkie's need to offer something new: there were plenty of Republicans prepared to assail the government, scarcely any who also endorsed a substantial social program. Later one might rationalize the exercise as a matter of Willkie's running with one party and wanting the votes of the other. But the best explanation is that Willkie continued to entertain both lines of thought. He knew that government could be oppressive, but in a time of depression he could think of virtually no program that he wished to eliminate. He could acclaim the merits of private enterprise and continue to hold the progressive suspicion of accumulated private power.

Willkie himself denied that there was a contradiction in his political philosophy. He was still a liberal, he repeatedly said, still a progressive, still interested above all in the protection of individual liberty. Only the problems had changed. "In the pre-war years we fought against domination of the people by Big Business. We now face the domination of the people by Big Government," he said in a speech at Indiana University. "The liberal will, of course, be sympathetic with the principles of much of the social legislation of recent years, but the liberal will also be on guard lest this trend go too far and suppress . . . individualism and initiative."[4]

The existence of two Willkies in the end probably helped the quest for the presidential nomination. Republicans of different views could pick the Willkie they wanted. It must be said, however, that he aroused the most excitement among centrist and left-of-center Republicans and progressive-minded businessmen. While Republicans on the right—the Old Guard, the harshest critics of expanded government activity—remained somewhat mystified, they reserved much room for skepticism about this new man.

By the spring of 1940 only eight or ten weeks remained before the Republicans would meet to pick a presidential candidate. The prospect that it would be Willkie seemed the most remote of possibilities; he was the darkest of dark horses. His name did not appear in opinion polls until April, then at the end of the month he received the support of only 3 percent of the people questioned. Only the most hopeful follower might have observed that forces favorable for a miracle had started to take shape.

By no means the least of these forces was the changing state of international affairs. The world in truth never had recovered from the Great War of 1914–1918. The Depression produced new international instability. By the start of 1940, Japan had been fighting

China for more than two years. If Americans found no direct threat in this distant Asian conflict, they could not ignore entirely Japanese advances over the hapless Chinese and the march of totalitarianism in an area that contained American possessions. Americans watched Europe with some detachment as well, as leaders there played out their hands. While determined to stay out of this wearisome European mess, Americans could take no comfort in watching the regime of Adolf Hitler take shape and the speed with which he established German dominance of Central Europe. With the outbreak of war in September 1939 a majority of Americans supported a shift from the cold and narrow isolationism of the mid-1930s to a position that would protect nonparticipation but still allow American neutrality to tilt toward Britain and France. Roosevelt's proposal to permit "cash and carry" sale of arms passed in November 1939 although without the votes of most Republicans. Then in April 1940, at the time Willkie was openly entering the presidential race, Hitler struck at western and northern Europe.

Establishing a position on the war in Europe centered on three propositions. First, to what extent should the United States favor the western allies at a risk of provoking Germany? That issue called to mind the experience of the First World War. Second, to what extent could policy be left in the hands of the president? If Roosevelt had been clear about his wish to assist Britain and France, he had been almost as emphatic in his intent to stay out of war. Many Republicans had no faith in anything he said. Third, to what extent were the security and general interests of the United States affected by the status of a conflict that in spring 1940 seemed to be changing almost daily?

The course of the European war cast new light on the men who had presented themselves for the Republican presidential nomination. It was not an outstanding group to begin with; none had well-established national reputations, and the demands of a world in crisis made the shortcomings of each all the more striking. Senator Arthur Vandenberg of Michigan, the early leader, had identified himself largely as an economic conservative and an isolationist, active in the effort in fall 1939 to prevent repeal of an embargo on sale of arms abroad. Losses in two presidential primaries placed him far behind, with little hope for victory beyond a deadlock of leading candidates. Senator Robert A. Taft of Ohio, son of a president, was a solid, loyal Republican, popular with party regulars, but weakened by a dour personality and a conservatism that attracted few followers beyond the political right. His preoccupation with domestic issues and failure to articulate a world view much beyond intending to avoid war seemed to place him out of touch with the dangerous environment of 1940.

That left Thomas E. Dewey of New York, the man in front. Only thirty-seven years old when he started running, Dewey probably would have won in spite of his age had the choice come a year earlier. He had had a dazzling career pursuing mobsters in New York and barely had missed winning the governorship. Still, the career seemed to dazzle more than the man, and even a marvelous speaking voice failed to generate much excitement. Though Dewey was surely less conservative than Taft and more of an internationalist than Taft or Vandenberg, it was difficult to know where he stood. He shifted frequently, evidently seeking to please everyone. The course of the war in 1940 gave more people cause to reconsider the wisdom of placing the government in the hands of a young county attorney.

Then, all of a sudden, there was Willkie. He emerged as something rare in politics, a competent person who also was colorful and exciting, the type one almost never found on the Republican side, with the possible exception of Theodore Roosevelt. Observers in New York had admired the intelligence and skill with which he had handled each stage of his career. Through it all he had acted with such good sense, such good humor and absence of meanness, that even his opponents had something good to say about him. This man of substance also possessed, as one person put it, "a personality to charm a bird from a tree, if he wanted to."[5]

What had started as a movement rooted in domestic issues and qualities of leadership blossomed quickly into a campaign also deeply involved in world affairs. Willkie had followed the war in Europe with close interest and made clear that the outcome was of great concern to the United States. While he expected that Americans would stay out of the fighting, he favored helping the enemies of Hitler in numerous ways. This position came easily to Willkie as an extension of his Wilsonism and of an internationalism that long had been at the core of his political philosophy. It also blended well with the basic premise on which Willkie had shifted parties. The totalitarianism of Hitler and Mussolini stood as the supreme expression of a threat from government that the Roosevelt administration—albeit on a lesser scale—presented to the United States.

Thus in foreign policy Willkie placed himself apart from others seeking the Republican nomination. The close support for Britain and France not only left him in step with most liberals; it was nearly identical to that of the Roosevelt administration. While this position did him no good with many Republican professionals, it seemed to be close to what the people were thinking. It also reaffirmed the idea of someone fresh to politics: a person who spoke his mind openly and honestly, even when it might carry no immediate reward.

In spring 1940 everything Willkie touched seemed to turn to gold. His brilliant performance on the popular radio show "Information Please" projected a man with broad knowledge and sharp wit, destined to take command. He enchanted Republican leaders with an extemporaneous speech in St. Paul. His article "We the People," published in *Fortune* in April, was a political manifesto that confirmed that two Willkies continued to exist. The essay, which, as one scholar put it, identified Willkie as "a low-tariff, anti-isolationist, Bill-of-Rights Democrat, in rebellion against the New Deal not because of its aims but because of its arbitrary exercise of power," inspired more prominent men to join the movement.[6] Young Oren Root, Jr., started the first of what would be hundreds of volunteer Willkie Clubs. Gardner and John Cowles, publishers of newspapers and *Look* magazine, came aboard, as did Henry Luce, owner of the enormous *Time-Life* empire. Davenport resigned from *Fortune* and became Willkie's campaign manager.

The strategy—to the extent there was one—was to project Willkie as the competent but unconventional outsider who said what he thought and knew what he was talking about. Imperfections of behavior stood as expressions of a man not afraid to let himself be known. There was no effort to hide the fact that he was a smoker—three packs a day, some said. He drank, too, and when angry could swear like a sailor. If by early afternoon a clump of hair fell carelessly over his forehead, his shirt had wilted and his suit looked as if he had slept in it, it was because this man worried about matters more important than personal appearance.

The objective was to present Willkie as a Hoosier rather than a New Yorker, the country boy, not the city slicker or corporation magnate. The corporation people already knew about Willkie. Being from Indiana seemed to carry a message about honesty, openness, and solid, down-home values. Fortunately Willkie almost personified the Hoosier (or rural) adage that "You can take the boy out of the country, but you cannot take the country out of the boy." He owned five farms in Rush County and visited them frequently. He never lost Hoosier laziness in speech: leaving out letters, chopping off syllables. The word *power*, for example, usually came out as "p'ar." He kept his hair parted and cut short on the side—country style, as they called it. "It's an asset . . . to look like an Indiana farmer," he once said.[7]

Aided by a remarkable publicity campaign, a barrage from nearly every leading national periodical, Willkie's popularity spread like wildfire. By the time the convention was ready to start in Philadelphia on June 24, the Gallup poll ranked him second behind Dewey. This popularity came with public opinion, however, not from Republican professionals or delegates to the convention. Among these people there remained much skepticism of Willkie's admitted liberalism and activism toward the war in Europe. Republicans, who might enjoy his eloquent defense of capitalism, might question the wisdom of running a man from a power company, in view of the greed and scandal recently associated with the utilities industry. The simplest reason for denying Willkie the nomination was that he had not earned it, that virtually all his life he had been a member of the other party, a position put most memorably by James E. Watson: "I don't mind the church converting a whore," said the former senator from Indiana, "but I don't like her to lead the choir the first night."[8]

Given the huge disadvantage with professionals, the Willkie campaign could go but one direction: to promote a grass-roots movement, or the appearance of one, a battle of a small man against the bosses. Whereas Taft's party reserved more than one hundred rooms at the convention and Dewey nearly eighty, Davenport set aside two small rooms at the Ben Franklin Hotel for his candidate. Willkie's name would be placed in nomination by a Hoosier, Congressman Charles A. Halleck. Arriving in Philadelphia, Willkie fell easily into stride. "Ask me any damn thing in the world," he said to reporters. "Nothing is off the record . . . , so shoot, ask anything you want." Speaking later to delegates, he said that "the big boys may . . . be hostile, but the man who works with his hands or wants to have a chance to get a job is rooting for me." At a chance meeting with Arthur Krock and Turner Catledge of the *New York Times,* Willkie claimed to have no organization, did not know what a floor manager was supposed to do. "If it's an act," wrote Krock, "it's a good one."[9]

The Republican convention that met in Philadelphia June 24–28 would be one of the most exciting in American political history. Joseph W. Martin, House minority leader and chair of the gathering, would call it the "greatest convention ever," and a half-century of politics since that time has produced nothing to challenge that claim.[10] A framework for the drama came with the fall of France the week before. Hitler had conquered western and central Europe; Britain was in deadly peril. The immediate source of the excitement that enveloped the Philadelphia delegates was a momentum for the nomination of Willkie. In the city and in the delegates' rooms and meeting places, Willkie (or how to stop Willkie) was virtually all one heard. Inside the hall the movement would dominate each session, with cries from the balconies of "We want Willkie" becoming so loud by Wednesday, the day of nominating speeches, that the convention barely could proceed. The steamroller moved steadily until the sixth ballot, when the candidate from Indiana went over the top. The Republicans had nominated a man with only the beginnings of a formal organization, a man who had conducted a campaign of only a few days. A party that was thought of as being conservative, anti–New Deal, and mostly isolationist selected a man who was liberal, almost a New Dealer, and an internationalist, a man who less than one year earlier had been registered as a Democrat. "Nothing so extraordinary has ever happened in American politics," said Harold L. Ickes, a member of Roosevelt's cabinet.[11]

For years to come the occasion would be remembered as "the miracle in Philadelphia."

Willkie's miracle stemmed from several forces, each related to the others, each probably necessary to bring about the remarkable outcome. First came a shortage of worthy alternative candidates, what Joseph Martin referred to as a vacuum of leadership within the party. The inability of anyone to win on an early ballot provided time for candidates farther back to pick up support. Favorite-son candidates from several states, a feature of politics in that age, helped deny anyone, particularly Dewey, an early victory.

The drastic turn in world events enlarged the vacuum. Dewey now seemed younger and more inexperienced than ever—some people quipped that he was the first American casualty of the war. Vandenberg and Taft seemed too shallow in their grasp of the war's meaning. Willkie by contrast appeared to be concrete, confident, and mature. His position made more sense during the convention than even two weeks earlier. His endorsement of aid to Hitler's enemies, of the need to resist brutality and totalitarianism, appeared to serve American interests and appealed to an individual's better instincts as well—no small factor when one is caught up in a movement. And, after all, Willkie argued that the United States should stay out of the fighting. He was no interventionist.

Willkie had support where and when it counted, either from professional politicians or professionals in other circles in a position to influence politics and politicians. The group included such people as John Hamilton, Pryor, Davenport, Luce, Sinclair Weeks, Bruce Barton, Governor Harold Stassen of Minnesota, and Governor Raymond Baldwin of Connecticut. The contributions ranged from mounting publicity campaigns of various kinds and packing galleries at the convention (the work of Pryor) to work on the floor at the time of balloting. Stassen managed a small group of operatives in the convention. Hamilton helped steer crucial shifts in the delegations of Kansas and Michigan.[12]

Willkie's victory also rested on widespread popular following. Admittedly, one cannot measure mood or the influence of a crowd the way one counts a shift in delegate voting. Professional politicians had some part in arranging the outburst in Philadelphia. Ability to rouse the rank and file was critical to Willkie's appeal—indeed, what he thought his candidacy was about—and a central part of his effort to capture delegate support. By taking over Philadelphia Willkie's people cast an impression that they could take the United States as well, that here was an electable candidate; their momentum influenced some delegates to do what with a few more days' sober reflection they might have decided not to do. If Willkie could not do without the Pryors and Stassens, he also had to have the likes of Oren Root, Jr., and the people in the balcony. One might imagine the outcome had crowds been shouting "We want Dewey." The magnet that drew these forces together, of course, was Willkie himself.

That the press approved of the decision at Philadelphia came as no surprise; the press, after all, helped nominate Willkie. What hardly could have been anticipated was a response from writers as well as editors that bordered on euphoria. Krock wrote of a "political revolution"; the *New York Times* called Willkie "head and shoulders above his rivals." "Right-minded, tough-minded, competent," said another writer, and the nomination was a "popular uprising of men and women who have responded as free people ought to respond." Walter Lippmann wrote that while Dewey and Taft sought to discover what voters wanted and follow them, Willkie believed that "a public man must express his conviction and then try to persuade the people to follow him." One view offered national policies, the other nothing more than popular promises. Fortunately the party that "for 18 months" had been "walking in its sleep" about world affairs awoke and picked a leader. The nomination of Willkie spared the country from "a disaster of disunion and demoralization," such a "competition in demagoguery" and "hysterical appeal to fear and selfishness" that the nation would have lost no matter which party won the election.[13]

Placed beside the magic of the nomination process, the campaign for election would have to be judged disappointing. Perhaps it could be no other way, for the sparkle of the nomination could not last forever. Instead of the dazzling march into politics with virtually nothing to lose and the crescendo at Philadelphia there would come many weeks of steady, grueling campaigning, with many bases to touch, many debts to pay, many opinions to hear. This time Willkie faced not young Tom Dewey but Franklin D. Roosevelt, the champ and master even with the warts accumulated from eight years in office. As presidential campaigns go, Willkie's could be labeled vigorous, exciting, even original in places. But as it went on it was plagued with error, more involved in demands—what could be taken as demands—of partisan politics, more given to expediency, even a touch of demagoguery. And of course it is impossible to evaluate a campaign without taking into account the outcome.

Willkie wanted to win the presidency the way he won the nomination—or the way he perceived having won it. He would lead a people's movement and people would vote for him because they could see he was no common politician but an open, honest man who knew how to care for his people and nation. Willkie expected to capitalize on his personal appeal—who could tell, after all, how far it extended?—show himself willing to break some rules of politics, depart from standard Republican rhetoric, even concede points to the opposition: all this consistent with a plan to offer something new to politics. "I will not talk in quibbling langauge," he said, "I will talk in simple, direct Indiana speech."[14] This approach also blended with a belief that Willkie did not need to woo the Republicans. He already had those votes, and there were not that many anyway. He would succeed by attracting Democrats and independents. He sought to win these votes by arguing that while government needed to care for the welfare of its people, Roosevelt's government had not done a good job of it, not with unemployment in 1940 at almost 15 percent. In the process of trying, the administration had caused much damage to private enterprise, had encroached on civil liberties, had become bloated, debt-ridden, arrogant, and power hungry. Why else would a president have the audacity to seek election a third consecutive time? Willkie knew that if the third term carried an aura of mystery and remained an issue never tested in American history, it provided a potential for widespread defection of people who had voted for Roosevelt twice.

Willkie approached the area of international affairs in much the same two-sided fashion. He wished to be open and honest, maintain principle and large objectives, even if they were the same as the administration, and at the same time explain why the people should elect him and not Roosevelt. The campaign of 1940 continued apace with the crisis in Europe. After the fall of France in June, Britain remained the sole obstacle to Hitler's mastery of the West. The air war over London—the Battle of Britain—competed daily with politics for attention in the American press. An invasion of the British Isles seemed imminent. In his contention that the security of the United States depended upon the survival of Britain, that Britain must have extensive American aid, Willkie took essentially the same course as the Roosevelt administration and apart from isolationists in the Republican party. He regarded his early endorsement of a law to draft men to military service another expression of honesty and principle. Coming against the advice of Martin (whom Willkie had selected as party chairman) and other Republicans who regarded it, if not bad policy, at least poor politics, Willkie's voluntary act eliminated a political issue and eased the task of the administration.

As with the attitude toward domestic problems, Willkie found more fault in the form and method of Roosevelt's foreign policy than in the major objectives. He complained about slowness and inefficiency in rebuilding the defense establishment. Before working out the controversial destroyer base deal with Winston Churchill in September, Roosevelt sought to recruit the support of Willkie, acting through Archibald MacLeish and William Allen White. Willkie sent word that while he favored Britain getting fifty American warships he would not give an open endorsement. When the exchange became public—a product of an executive agreement—Willkie yielded to advisers and denounced the move as the most "dictatorial action ever taken by any president."[15] Willkie found a close connection between shortcomings in foreign policy and the conduct of government in general. "Only the strong can be free, and only the productive can be strong" became the catchword of the campaign.

The campaign had little more than started when it began to encounter problems, many of them attributable to the candidate's determination to do things his way, at the expense of conventional political wisdom. Willkie spoke too often, too long, and too loud and temporarily lost his voice. His reliance upon amateurs, notably Davenport and Root, provoked Republican professionals and caused much tension on the campaign trail. He issued potentially offensive impromptu remarks that careful monitoring might have prevented. That these moves represented mistakes there can be little doubt, especially in view of the fact that he lost. With more thought Willkie would not have shouted "To hell with Chicago" when he appeared in suburban Cicero. To Republican regulars these mistakes constituted the reason for defeat. That they cost many votes, that they subtracted more than was added by the spirit of freshness and originality that produced them, is doubtful.

Failure to find a focus stemmed from the fact that the two Willkies continued to exist: Willkie the corporation executive and now Republican candidate and Willkie the liberal and former Democrat. He could offer sharp criticism of government competition with private enterprise, of too much regulation and too much spending, and end up endorsing most of the legislation that had produced these problems. Norman Thomas summed up one major speech with the comment that Willkie "agreed with Mr. Roosevelt's entire program of social reform and said it was leading to disaster."[16] For all the criticism of Roosevelt's conduct of diplomacy, his failure in promoting defense of the United States, Willkie endorsed at least as much aid for Britain as the president, with all the risks the policy carried. According to Robert E. Sherwood, Roosevelt's speech writer: "What Willkie was saying, in effect, was, 'you can trust me to do the same thing, only better' or as the more embittered members of the Republican Old Guard put it, 'me too.' "[17]

And of course the Democrats did not leave the campaign entirely up to the opposition. Roosevelt had based a controversial and risky quest for a third term on the premise that the international crisis justified a move that otherwise would be unthinkable. Consistent with that logic and with a plan to exploit the prestige of his office, Roosevelt said he would not campaign. He did hold himself ready to point out "deliberate or unwitting falsification of fact." The president also planned to make numerous short "nonpolitical" inspection trips to defense establishments in the East.[18]

Meanwhile other Democratic spokesmen revealed a strategy of identifying Willkie as business tycoon from New York rather than honest Indiana farmer and holding him accountable for the least attractive features of his new party. Speaking sarcastically about the "simple, barefoot Wall Street lawyer," Ickes referred to Willkie as a utilities magnate and bank director with connections to the firm of J. P. Morgan. Other attacks came from such politicians as Henry A. Wallace, the vice-presidential nominee; Ed Flynn, Democratic national chairman; and Governor Herbert H. Lehman of New York. The thesis of this somewhat dubious pitch was to mark the Republicans with irresponsible isolationism and imply that because Roosevelt was "the man that Hitler wants to see defeated," the Nazis supported Willkie. Wallace in September charged that while "every Republican is not an appeaser . . . , you can be sure that every Nazi, every Hitlerite and every appeaser is a Republican." *Time* reported that the campaign had become a contest between Roosevelt and Hitler "with Willkie a poor third."[19]

He was losing. Despite vigorous campaigning across the country outside the South, despite enthusiastic crowds and evidence that the old magnetism still existed, he was losing ground. Roosevelt ignored his opponent, busied himself with being president and commander-in-chief, visiting factories but making no "political" speeches. He was gaining in the polls, and the margin widened as the contest entered its last month.

Frustrated with an inability to engage his illusive opponent, angered and hurt at dirty Democratic tactics—the effort to link him to Hitler, aspersions to his German background, even hints about a racist upbringing—Willkie in October stepped up his assaults. Now he equated the "Mr. Third Term" candidacy with bossism and dictatorial practices in the Democratic party and Roosevelt's government. Most important, he accused Roosevelt of deliberately leading the country into war. When the charge seemed to catch on and reinvigorate the campaign, Willkie kept up the attack to the finish, predicting at the end of October that with the president remaining in office, the country would be at war by April of the following year.

The last phase of the campaign scarcely represented Willkie at his best. It was marked by expediency, using the tactic of fear, and constituted a concession to the Old Guard, if not the isolationists. To Willkie's fondest supporters it represented an unfortunate diversion from what otherwise had been a crusade based on principle, courage, and determination to tell the truth. To critics in either party it tarnished Willkie's claim to originality and moral superiority. The tactic did frighten Roosevelt and the people around him, causing the president to enter the campaign abruptly and make some highly quotable statements about his intent to keep the nation at peace. If Willkie's aggressive campaigning seemed to produce a turn toward the Republicans in the polls, it of course stopped short of victory. It is doubtful that introducing the strategy earlier would have made a difference. When the campaign had ended, Roosevelt's margin stood at ten points, almost as large as at any time.

The outcome thus was not close. Roosevelt carried thirty-eight states with 449 electoral votes, 55 percent of the popular vote. Willkie had ten states with eighty-two votes in the electoral college, 45 percent of the popular vote. Willkie nonetheless had done much better than challengers in the two previous elections, better than Dewey would do in two future contests with Roosevelt and Harry S. Truman. A measure of the distance Willkie had come might be noted in the fact that he carried Indiana by almost 25,000 votes, a state that Roosevelt had won in the previous election by 243,000. He would take most satisfaction in his effort to take the Republican party along a new and in his judgment more positive and responsible course. He was the most attractive and inspiring Republican candidate during a quarter century of Democrat dominance of presidential politics.

Explanations of the outcome of the election of 1940 differed with perspective. Many Republican stalwarts complained about a campaign that was neither as Republican nor as professional as it needed to be, leading to an absence of sharpened issues—except perhaps in the final stages—and without full participation of seasoned professionals. The charges have some basis in fact; what is uncertain is that a tidier, more partisan and professional campaign would have changed the outcome, given the reasons people voted as they did. Blurred issues were a consequence of Willkie's liberalism and of a design to win by attracting people who previously had voted Democratic. Urging people to vote Republican was not enough. Tightening of organization would have conflicted with the basic theme—

and perhaps greatest appeal—of Willkie's campaign as a people's movement that superceded traditional rules of politics.

Willkie lost because he had too far to come, too many voters to convert, especially in the exceptional circumstances of 1940. Roosevelt won because he had built up a considerable reservoir of strength, particularly with low-income voters, and because he could lay claim to experience in handling national affairs in a time of crisis. With no effort at all he could count on support from all the southern states. Willkie based his hope for success on his personal appeal and a negative reaction to ineffective policies and Roosevelt's willingness to seek a third term. The outcome depended more on the appeal of Roosevelt. To the small person he appeared as a leader who cared, even though he had not delivered very much. Even Willkie's recruitment of John L. Lewis, president of the CIO, did little to produce a shift in working-class votes. The negative response to the third term—which did indeed exist—was softened by Roosevelt's claim to sound and seasoned leadership in a world at war.

Americans in 1940 voted for Roosevelt more than they voted against his opponent. Willkie, many Democrats believed, could have defeated any Democrat but Roosevelt. He might have defeated Roosevelt except for the war. Except for the war, however, Roosevelt surely would not have been a candidate for the presidency and neither, probably, would Willkie.

Willkie's participation in politics of course did not end with the election of 1940. For a man of his position and caliber everything he did would have political implication. Legions of loyal followers stood ready at almost a moment's notice to begin the next campaign. In a national address a week after the election—an exceptional move for a defeated candidate—Willkie exhibited the grace and good-headedness his friends had come to admire. He requested support for the president in the difficult times ahead and promised to represent the loyal opposition.

In months to come he behaved more loyally than in opposition, or so it seemed to other Republican leaders. He rejected advice to expand on attacks begun in the campaign—on presidential dictatorship, for example, and warmongering—and instead virtually apologized for charges made during the campaign. He openly and actively supported Roosevelt's lend-lease bill, a proposal that Republicans fought tooth and nail. His visit to Britain in early 1941, though a private undertaking, carried the president's blessing. For his heralded world trip in 1942 Roosevelt provided a B-24 bomber and Willkie traveled as the president's personal representative. His speech to the nation on return and publication in 1943 of his remarkably successful *One World* stood as a ringing assertion that isolationism had no place in the world of the future, if not an endorsement of basic policies of the Roosevelt administration.

While these moves produced new rounds of acclaim for patriotism, perception, and broadmindedness and for Willkie's new dimensions of competence, they also inspired an undying hostility in Republicans still given to isolationism and traditional notions of partisan politics. Being on the outside is always uncomfortable in a time of war, when pressure to support the government clashes with a natural inclination to attack the opposition. What Willkie viewed as good sense and in the interests of the United States, showing the way his party ought to go, many Republicans interpreted as pursuing wrong policies and fostering the welfare of the Democratic party to boot.

It is somewhat surprising in this state of affairs that Willkie concluded he could win the Republican presidential nomination in 1944. His behavior suggests that whatever he had learned since becoming a national figure, the art of American politics was not part of it. He evidently failed to distinguish between what appeared to be the popular mood in the country and the attitude of people who counted in the selection of candidates. In this context he might have listened to his friend from Indiana, Homer Capehart. "The public is with you," wrote Capehart in 1943. "The professional politician is against you."[20] Willkie functioned out of a conviction that this was a time of new politics as well as new policies and that competence and dedication to purpose would win out in the end, even in the Republican party. After all, there was still the memory of the miracle at Philadelphia.

And so run for the nomination he did, openly, vigorously, for more than a year. His challengers included Stassen and General Douglas MacArthur, but most important Dewey, who by this time was governor of New York. Many Republicans, however, seemed more interested in defeating Willkie than in supporting someone else. The primary basis for opposition, according to Willkie's loyal friend and supporter Gardner Cowles, was that many Republicans regarded Willkie as "a carbon copy of Roosevelt."[21]

Willkie's response was to sharpen his positions, seeking to bring people to his thinking rather than moving over to what many perceived as mainstream Republican thought. He called for destruction of "isolationism, ultranationalism," supported close cooperation with the Soviet Union and an international organization, favored a program of "liberal progressive ideas" at home, and promised to appoint a black person to his cabinet. He challenged his critics, either by name or by implication, and engaged in several heated confrontations. It was honest, even courageous, but scarcely practical, given the mechanics of politics in the 1940s. As Sherwood wrote: "Greatly as the Old Guard lords of the Republican machine hated Roosevelt, they had come to hate Willkie even more, and be it to his eternal credit, Willkie went out of his way to court their hatred."[22]

Faced with such hostility among party regulars and with the growing strength of Dewey, Willkie entered primaries in the few states that had them, seeking to demonstrate popularity among the rank and file. To supporters who had come to see futility in the effort, Willkie promised to quit if he did not win in Wisconsin in April. A state with a considerable progressive tradition but also a large German population and deep roots in isolationism, within easy reach of Colonel Robert McCormick's *Chicago Tribune,* Wisconsin seemed to symbolize the huge task before him. He devoted two weeks to intensive campaigning in the state. While no other contender appeared, Dewey, Stassen, and MacArthur had people working on their behalf. The result was a shocker, from everyone's perspective. Dewey won seventeen delegates, Stassen four, MacArthur three; Willkie received none. He pulled out of the race the next day.

He did not sulk, even after the Republicans shut him out of their activities. He was not permitted to participate in the national convention. Report and rumor followed through the summer of 1944: Willkie was to buy a newspaper; he would take a job in Roosevelt's government and run with the president on the Democratic ticket; he would endorse Roosevelt or endorse Dewey, who had won the Republican nomination. Most intriguing was a scheme to join with Roosevelt in some form of future political realignment—possibly the creation of a new party of liberals. Although the project became stalled in the complexities of a presidential race, both men were interested in continuing a discussion and had exchanged several communications. Only fifty-two years old, Willkie appeared to have numerous options at his choosing, and anything but participation in policy at the highest level would have been a betrayal of his talents and ambition. His death on October 8, 1944, diminished the quality of politics in the United States.

He left a mark. For years to come politicians on both sides would remark about the spark he gave their profession. While many of them found inspiration in his dogged idealism and honesty, they probably learned as much from Willkie about the need to pay attention to housekeeping requirements of party politics. He earned an admiration rarely afforded losers in American politics—a sharp contrast, for example, with the treatment given to Dewey, to Richard Nixon in 1960, and to Michael Dukakis in 1988. His contribution to internationalism and a bipartisan foreign policy has been noted by scholars of the Roosevelt era. His was probably the most eloquent voice at the time for full-scale participation by the United States in the affairs of the world. He gave at least a measure of Republican sanction to the New Deal. His ideas about social and economic policies were too pronounced for many Republicans, but he at least articulated the need for something beyond the negativism of the Old Guard and gave expression to a point of view that would be identified as moderate, modern, or liberal Republicanism. When a Republican victory at last did come with the election of Dwight Eisenhower in 1952, it relied heavily on Willkie's approach, stressing the candidate's personal popularity and appealing to the political center. The line from Willkie to Eisenhower can be spotted immediately. Even Dewey in 1944 proclaimed himself an internationalist.

The most enduring memory of Willkie the politician is of Willkie the presidential candidate in 1940, for it is here that his impact was at the same time most concrete and most inspiring. His internationalist posture, as Lippmann wrote, spared the United States a sharp division over foreign policy. No less a person than Roosevelt suggested that such policies as conscription—and later, lend-lease—might not have been possible without Willkie's support. His shift in the final stages of the campaign represented an appeal to isolationists but not an appeal to isolationism. His candidacy denied isolationism the most powerful forum it could have had in the period before the United States entered the Second World War.

Then there is the romantic vision of this huge man with the rumpled clothes and clump of hair falling over the right side of his forehead, sounding like a bullfrog but projecting the notion that in the end it is substance not form that counts. And there was the magical spring of 1940, the dash to the nomination, the thunderous shouts of "We want Willkie"—and up there, waving from the podium in Philadelphia, stood visible proof that through determination, holding to the faith, and being right the little people after all do have a chance.

NOTES

1. Roscoe Drummond, "Wendell Willkie: A Study in Courage," Isabel Leighton, ed., *The Aspirin Age, 1919–1941* (New York, 1949), 447.

2. See Steve Neal, *Dark Horse: A Biography of Wendell Willkie* (New York, 1984), 15–24.

3. *New York Times,* February 22, 1939; *Fortune,* May 1937, 83.

4. Wendell L. Willkie, *This Is Wendell Willkie* (New York, 1940), 165–66.

5. Neal, *Dark Horse,* 52.

6. Ellsworth Barnard, *Wendell Willkie: Fighter For Freedom* (Marquette, Mich., 1966), 154.

7. Cited in Donald B. Johnson, *The Republican Party and Wendell Willkie* (Urbana, Ill., 1960), 54.

8. There are several versions of this popular remark. This one comes from Mary Earhart Dillon, *Wendell Willkie, 1892–1944* (New York, 1952), 143.

9. Neal, *Dark Horse*, 87, 96; Arthur Krock, *Memoirs: Sixty Years on the Firing Line* (New York, 1968), 194.

10. Joseph W. Martin, "The Greatest Convention Ever: I Remember Willkie," *Saturday Evening Post*, July 9, 1960, 21–22, 80–82.

11. Harold L. Ickes, *The Secret Diary of Harold L. Ickes*, vol. 3, *The Lowering Clouds, 1939–1941* (New York, 1954), 221.

12. For a discussion of the role of professionals in Willkie's nomination, see Hugh Ross, "Was the Nomination of Wendell Willkie a Political Miracle?" *Indiana Magazine of History*, June 1962, 79–100.

13. *New York Times*, June 28 and 30, 1940; *Evansville Courier*, June 24 and 26, July 3 and August 21, 1940.

14. Neal, *Dark Horse*, 143.

15. *New York Times*, September 7, 1940.

16. Neal, *Dark Horse*, 136.

17. Robert E. Sherwood, *Roosevelt and Hopkins: An Intimate History* (New York, 1948), 184–85.

18. James M. Burns, *Roosevelt: The Lion and the Fox* (New York, 1956), 433–37.

19. *New York Times*, August 30 and September 10, 1940; *Time*, September 9, 1940, 15.

20. Homer Capehart to Wendell L. Willkie, February 13, 1943, Wendell L. Willkie Papers, Lilly Library, Indiana University, Bloomington.

21. Gardner Cowles, Jr., to Willkie, January 21, 1944, Willkie Papers.

22. Sherwood, *Roosevelt and Hopkins*, 830–31.

HARVARD SITKOFF

Willkie as Liberal

CIVIL LIBERTIES & CIVIL RIGHTS

THERE IS LITTLE agreement among historians and biographers of Wendell Willkie as to why he became one of the most ardent, outspoken champions of civil rights and civil liberties of his era. Some attribute his concern for the underdog to the influence of his mother, Henrietta Trisch Willkie, the first woman admitted to the Indiana bar and a fiercely independent battler for her beliefs. Some stress the importance of his father, Herman, Elwood's legal defender of the controversial and unorthodox, a lover of justice and pro-Bryan Democrat who had once joined the Socialist party. And some see the roots of his later beliefs in the youthful experiences of a second-generation American acutely aware of the difficulties faced by minorities in a conformist society. Others see the genesis of the mature Willkie's views in his early idolization of Robert M. La Follette, Sr., or enthusiasm for Wilsonian liberalism. Still others explain his highly unconventional defense of unpopular causes as a manifestation of Willkie's guilt over his extraordinary financial success as a corporate attorney or as an indication of a maverick, volatile personality courting political suicide. Contrarily, some describe his tireless promotion of racial equality during the Second World War as political expediency, a deliberate bid to woo African-American voters. What some term intellectual growth, the emerging conviction that the defeat of the Axis and the creation of a just and lasting peace required ending racial imperialism at home as well as abroad, others see as psychological need, a gadfly desperate to irritate the complacent, to sting the conservatives of both major political parties.

Whatever the cause, however, none doubt that Wendell Willkie became a passionate exponent of freedom, justice, and democracy. More than any other presidential contender in his time, the rumpled Hoosier dramatically decried prejudice and intolerance. In an unmistakable Indiana twang, Willkie eloquently restated the American creed, sounding the call of equal rights and equal opportunities for all. Some two decades ahead of most of the American people and their political representatives, Willkie openly sided with African Americans in their struggle against discrimination.

Growing up in Elwood, Indiana, a town that had no African-American residents but might well have had a sign proclaiming "Nigger, don't let the sun go down on you here," the young Willkie had little opportunity to exhibit signs of racial liberalism. Later, as a student at Indiana University, Willkie devoted most of his political energies to espousing Wilsonian ideals of international cooperation. The first indication of his pronounced opposition to bigotry did not come until he was a successful lawyer in his early thirties. In 1924 he attended the Democratic National Convention as a delegate from Akron, Ohio, in order, he claimed, "to put the Democratic party on record against the Ku Klux Klan." The following year he played a prominent role in opposing the KKK in Akron politics.[1] As an ambitious business attorney, however, Willkie never sought to represent minorities or unpopular causes, and when he gained fame and fortune as the head of Commonwealth and Southern during the 1930s Willkie never decried the widespread discrimination against African Americans in the public utilities industry.[2]

Similarly, the hero of Wall Street, the frequent critic of President Franklin D. Roosevelt for the New Deal's excessive spending and concentration of too much power in Washington, only belatedly and gradually became a vocal defender of civil liberties. Following Commonwealth and Southern's victory over the Tennessee Valley Authority and Willkie's first cover story in *Time* as the kind of liberal nonpolitician that the nation needed, he lashed out against the House Un-American Activities Committee (HUAC) in an address to the alumni of Columbia University in November 1939. Known as the Dies committee after its chair, Martin Dies of Texas, HUAC had been established in 1938; its sensationalized public hearings quickly became a forum for wild allegations of communist influence and control, particularly against liberals in the labor movement and in New Deal agencies. Willkie was especially disturbed by the abuses of due process and of the First Amendment in congressional investigations, by their scapegoating tactics and casual charges of conspiracy, and by their use of exposure simply for the sake of exposure. He specifically attacked legislative investigations in which witnesses were without the protection of counsel and denied the right to rebut charges or cross-examine their accusers. Willkie concluded his speech with a sharp critique of the Dies committee's employment of innuendo and inference in publicity to destroy reputations.[3]

Willkie repeated these charges in a March 1940 article in the *New Republic*. Entitled "Fair Trial," the article called for "equal treatment for all under law." It condemned punishing people for their political opinions, asserting that Eugene Debs had been indicted under the Espionage Act and Huey Long had been hounded by the Internal Revenue Service because political authorities wanted them out of the way. In like manner, Willkie wrote, the German-American Bund leader Fritz Kuhn and the Communist Earl Browder were now being denied due process because of their political beliefs. "Equal treatment under the law means exactly what it says," Willkie asserted, "whether the man before the tribunal is a crook, a Democrat, a Republican, a Communist, or a businessman; whether he is rich or poor, white or black, good or bad. You cannot have a democracy on any other basis. Those who truly believe in the protection of civil liberties," he continued, "will wonder whether Browder was sentenced to four years in jail and a $2,000 fine because he made a false statement on a passport application or because he was a Communist party member." Articulating a theme he would frequently repeat in the next four years, Willkie proclaimed: "It is well to remember that any man who denies justice to someone he hates prepares the way for a denial of justice to someone he loves."[4]

Following his nomination for the presidency by the Republican party in 1940, the former utility tycoon exhibited more passion in his defense of civil liberties and the rights of African Americans. Stung by the label affixed to him by Harold Ickes—"the simple, barefoot Wall Street lawyer"—and by Alice Roosevelt Longworth's taunt that his nomination "comes right from the grass roots of every country club in America," Willkie courted the support of prominent civil libertarians and civil rights leaders. With much fanfare he rejected the support of Father Charles Coughlin and the endorsement "of anybody else who stands for any form of prejudice as to anybody's race or religion. I don't have to be President of the United States," he added, "but I do have to live with myself." Still, wanting very much to be president, Willkie made a major effort to recapture the votes of the many African Americans who had deserted the GOP and switched to the Democratic party with the coming of the New Deal. He understood that he would have to work especially hard to win the support of African Americans who had been directly assisted by the New Deal's relief programs and had come to admire, even love, the president and first lady.[5]

"There is no man more opposed to racial discrimination," Willkie told a group of African-American reporters at the Republican nominating convention in Philadelphia. "If I am elected president I will seek to remove all kinds of discrimination from all kinds of groups." He claimed proudly that the Republicans had invited a larger number of African-American delegates to the convention than ever before and that they had written into the party platform the strongest civil rights plank in the nation's history, vigorously endorsing federal antilynching legislation and protection of the African American's right to vote and pledging that "discrimination in the civil service, army, navy, and all other branches of the government must cease." Going even further, Willkie also promised to end racial discrimination in the nation's capital.[6] Willkie's appeals to African Americans during the campaign earned him the support of the two largest Negro newspapers, the *Pittsburgh Courier* and *Baltimore Afro-American,* and forced President Roosevelt to reassure civil rights leaders of his concern in order to stop a mass defection of black voters to the GOP. In a series of announcements shortly before the election the president promoted an African-American colonel to the rank of brigadier general, appointed a prominent NAACP attorney as a special aide to the secretary of war, created the new post of Negro adviser to the director of selective service, and vowed that African Americans would be fully included in the armed forces and in defense employment. These moves enabled Roosevelt to retain the lion's share of the African-American vote in 1940 and convinced Willkie of the necessity to continue fighting for civil rights. The combination of political expediency and conviction led him to announce after his defeat that he would continue his battle for racial equality, civil rights, and the brotherhood of man.[7]

In 1941 Willkie plunged into the role of constructive critic of the Roosevelt administration and titular leader of the Republicans, especially those GOP liberals struggling to wrest the party away from its reactionaries. Despite denunciations from those such as conservative Republican Congressman Dewey Short of Missouri, who labeled him "Wee Windy War Willkie," a "bellowing, blatant, bellicose, belligerent, bombastic, bombinating, blowhard," the burley Hoosier railed against the forces of isolationism and intolerance. When a special subcommittee of the Senate Committee on Interstate Commerce launched an investigation of "war propaganda disseminated by the motion picture industry," Willkie agreed to serve as counsel for the Hollywood studio heads. With the same flair for dramatizing an issue and for gaining favorable publicity that he had shown in the fight against the TVA, Willkie went on the offensive, insisting on the movie industry's right of free speech. He demolished the charges of Democratic isolationist Bennett Champ Clark and Republican firebrands Gerald Nye and Burton Wheeler that Hollywood was "warmongering" and campaigning for aid to Great Britain, and converted the issue from propaganda for war to freedom from federal censorship. Following the collapse of the hearings, Willkie became chairman of the board of Twentieth-Century Fox and used that office to plead that the film industry "break the accepted Hollywood stereotype of the Negro as a buffoon, a servant, or a minstrel."[8]

As the United States drew closer to war, moreover, Willkie stepped up his attacks on the bigots in the Republican party. He accused

Charles Lindbergh and his followers of anti-Semitism, insisting in September 1941 that if "the American people permit race prejudice to arise at this crucial moment, they little deserve to preserve democracy."[9] In November he became a member of the American Bar Association's Committee on the Bill of Rights, and shortly after, in a speech to the National Conference of Christians and Jews, he pledged to lead the fight against intolerance: "In the courtroom and from the public rostrum, I will fight for the preservation of civil liberties, no matter how unpopular the cause may be in any given instance."[10]

True to his vow but against the urgings of his closest political advisers, who feared adverse consequences, Willkie agreed to act as counsel for a Communist party official in California, William Schneiderman, who was fighting the revocation of his naturalized citizenship. Two lower federal courts had already concurred with the 1939 decision of the Immigration and Naturalization Service of the Department of Labor that Schneiderman's citizenship should be revoked, and the announcement that Willkie would handle the Communist's appeal to the Supreme Court was front-page news and an affront to many Republicans. Nevertheless, in a letter to his friend Bartley Crum, Willkie wrote, "I am sure I am right in representing Schneiderman. Of all the times when civil liberties should be defended, it is now."[11] He later recalled:

> I saw myself as the man involved in the case. . . . While I did not agree with his views, he was entitled to them and to a fair trial under our system, and to the safeguards of our constitution. He had arrived in this predicament by a series of accidents of life. I had started as he had from pretty much the same point of thinking. My series of personal accidents had taken me down an opposite road. They might well have been different, and if they had I might now be in his predicament and in such event I would have wanted the type of representation and advocacy that satisfied me.[12]

Willkie pleaded Schneiderman's case before the Supreme Court in November 1942, shortly after returning from his trip around the world, and at a rehearing the following March. The government contended that the Russian-born Schneiderman had concealed his membership in the Communist party when he applied for citizenship in 1927 and that because the party then "believed in, advocated, and taught the overthrow of this government by force and violence," Schneiderman had failed to meet the requirement of the Naturalization Act passed by Congress in 1906 that an applicant for citizenship must believe in "the principles of the Constitution." Willkie countered that the individual liberty of an American citizen, and not the Communist party, was on trial, and claimed that the lower court decisions constituted "a drastic abridgement of freedom of political belief and thought." He asked the justices, "Am I to be held responsible for everything Ham Fish says?" emphasizing that the principles of a political party were not fully accepted by all of its members. In addition, quoting Jefferson and Lincoln, Willkie stated that these founders of the Democratic and Republican parties had been more forceful than even Karl Marx in advocating the use of violence when other methods failed. Five justices accepted Willkie's argument. Ruling in Schneiderman's favor, the Supreme Court repudiated the idea of guilt by association. The burden of proof, it affirmed, must be on the government to show that an individual personally advocated illegal doctrines. "Under our traditions," Justice Frank Murphy wrote for the court majority, "beliefs are personal and not a matter of mere association. Men in adhering to a political party or other organization notoriously do not subscribe to all of its platforms or asserted principles." In addition, Murphy opined, "There is a material difference between agitation and exhortation calling for present violent action which creates a clear and present danger of public disorder . . . and mere doctrinal justification or prediction of the use of force under hypothetical conditions at some indefinite future time." The Schneiderman decision would later be used to stop the government's efforts to deport various radicals and Communists, including Harry Bridges, the Australian-born head of the West Coast leftist longshoremen's union. A grateful Bridges told reporters that "Wendell Willkie was the only man in America who has proved that he would rather be right than be President." Conversely, Republican Paul Shafer of Michigan castigated Willkie on the floor of the House of Representatives for doing more to aid the Communists that he did for the GOP.[13]

Indeed, conservatives in both major parties considered Willkie's activities and pronouncements in 1942 anathema. His blunt assaults on bigotry and slashing attacks on colonialism at home and abroad provoked their mounting enmity. Yet Willkie stuck to his principles. He defended all Americans of alien descent, asserting that the nation's strength came from its myriad of "races, colors and creeds," and that "no American has the right to impugn the patriotism of any other American because of the accident of his birth or race or religion." Alluding to the forced removal of Japanese Americans from the West Coast, Willkie announced: "I have no trust and faith in any extra-judicial proceedings under which any group will be deprived of their rights, under guise of war emergency." "It is the right of every citizen in America," he frequently told reporters, "to be treated by other citizens as an equal. Our liberties are the equal rights of every citizen."[14] Again and again he urged his followers to guard against, and to act against, prejudice. "We cannot allow whispers about Jews, or Catholics, or Negroes, or any other groups, to spread through our ranks. We cannot, above all, allow whispers, rumors, slanders and the like, to cause us to ACT against our fellow citizens."[15] To rebut a *Saturday Evening Post* article by Milton Mayer that Willkie considered a "flagellation of the Jews," he wrote "The Case for the Minorities" for the same magazine. He decried the revival "of age-old racial and religious distrusts," and the demagogic scapegoating of minorities. He denounced discrimination in industry and labor and described being "appalled at the callous indifference of high officers of the Navy to the obvious and undemocratic discrimination against Negroes." And movingly he warned of the dangers of a wartime "period that is psychologically susceptible to witch-hanging and mob-baiting. And each of us, if not alert, may find himself the unconscious carrier of the germ that will destroy our freedom. For each of us has within himself the inheritance of age-long hatreds, of racial and religious differences, and everyone has a tendency to find the cause for his own failures in some conspiracy of evil."[16]

For his "unstinting devotion to the cause of democracy, freedom, oppressed minorities, tolerance and better understanding in America," Willkie received the American Hebrew medal for 1942. He used the occasion to proselytize for democratic equality rather than "tolerance." "No man has the right in America to treat any other man 'tolerantly,' for 'tolerance' is the assumption of superiority. Our liberties are the equal rights of every citizen." As never before, moreover, Willkie in 1942 wholly identified himself with the African-American struggle against racial discrimination and for equal opportunities. Particularly incensed by the "discrimination and the mistreatment" African Americans suffered in the armed forces, Willkie enlisted in their "fight for the right to fight." "They should have the right of every citizen to fight for his country," Willkie forthrightly declared, "in any branch of her armed forces without discrimination."[17] In an address to Freedom House in March he recalled the heroism of Dorrie Miller, a black mess attendant, during the attack on Pearl Harbor, and lamented that Miller "cannot enlist in the United States Navy, and only for the reason that he was born with a black skin." Angrily, Willkie called upon his audience to "correct this injustice . . . which makes a mockery of all our fine words."[18] In part because of his pronounced support for the African-American "double V" campaign—victory over the Axis abroad and over Jim Crow at home—some of the barriers against blacks in the military were breached during the Second World War.

Willkie and his African-American allies would have less success, although not for want of trying, in diminishing Hollywood's stereotyping of blacks as superstitious buffoons or primitive barbarians, as docile slaves or ignorant servants incapable of anything but the most menial tasks. Willkie's concern that the motion picture industry exhibit greater racial sensitivity deepened as his relationship with Walter White blossomed. Favoring Roosevelt in 1940, the executive secretary of the National Association for the Advancement of Colored People (NAACP) had spurned Willkie's entreaties for a meeting during the campaign. Shortly after the defeat, however, the two accidentally met at a dinner at New York's Waldorf-Astoria and quickly began what White would later describe as one of "the

closest and richest friendships of my life." They visited one another
frequently, talked incessantly about the varieties of racial oppression,
and, usually over their double Scotches, mapped strategies to up-
grade the status of African Americans. Appointed a special counsel
to the NAACP, Willkie joined White in Hollywood in 1941 to discuss with studio executives their derogatory treatment of African
Americans in the movies. Gaining little but vague promises, the two
returned to Hollywood the following year. They pleaded with industry leaders to depict "the Negro as a normal human being and
an integral part of human life and activity," and pointed out the
offensiveness of racial stereotyping and the harm it did to the war
effort. In a fiery, uncompromising speech to a largely Jewish group
of film directors and producers, Willkie reminded them "that they
should be the last to be guilty of doing to another minority what
has been done to them." The two continued their campaign for
better screen roles for blacks at the Writers' Congress in Los Angeles
in 1943. That year, such films as *Casablanca* and *The Ox-Bow Incident*
included a more favorable depiction of blacks than before. "But with
the tragedy of Willkie's death in 1944," White recorded in his
memoirs, "most of those responsible in Hollywood for changing
the pattern appeared to feel that the pressure upon them had been
removed." The "new concept of the Negro" that Willkie and White
had pressed for did not materialize.[19]

The Hollywood campaign was but one of the many battles for
civil rights that Willkie fought during the war. For him, racism had
become a national dilemma, a hindrance to United States foreign
and military policies. "It is becoming apparent to thoughtful Americans that we cannot fight the forces of imperialism abroad and maintain a form of imperialism at home," he thundered to an audience
at the NAACP's annual conference in 1942. Nevertheless, he continued, we practice "race imperialism" every day. "The attitude of
white citizens toward the Negroes has undeniably had some of the
unlovely and tragic characteristics of an alien imperialism—a smug
racial superiority, a willingness to exploit an unprotected people.
Our very proclamations of what we are fighting for have rendered
our own inequities self-evident. When we talk of freedom and op-

portunity for all nations, the increasing paradoxes in our own society become so clear they can no longer be ignored."[20]

Willkie reiterated this call to end the internal colonization of African Americans in greater detail in "Our Imperialism at Home," a
chapter in his best-selling and widely condensed and digested *One
World* (1943). Relating how often Arabs and Asians asked him
about race relations in the United States, Willkie warned of the adverse consequences that result from mistreatment of African Americans. "We cannot be on one side abroad and the other at home,"
he wrote; if we are to demand the British liberation of India we
must "make all who live in America free." Challenging Americans
to end their racism, Willkie insisted that hundreds of millions of
nonwhites around the globe will be judging us on the basis of our
racial practices and that the future peace and security of the nation
require a cessation of "race imperialism" within the United States.[21]

Legitimized by such expressions, and by similar ones from such
prominent whites as Eleanor Roosevelt and Vice-President Henry
Wallace, civil rights leaders and their organizations forcefully demanded equality on the battlefront and on the home front. Unlike
their counterparts during World War I, few African-American leaders in the Second World War asked blacks to close ranks and ignore
their grievances until the war ended. Rather, the very dependency
of the government on the loyalty and cooperation of African Americans intensified their insistence on "Democracy in Our Time!" And
the more African Americans saw racial barriers begin to be toppled,
the more militantly they pressed for the total and speedy dismantling
of the entire Jim Crow system. The explosive combination of ac-
celerating African-American expectations of change and the slow
pace of actual racial progress clashed head-on in 1943 with the
equally explosive fear and anger of whites throughout the United
States to "keep the niggers in their place." An epidemic of racial
conflict resulted: hate strikes against the hiring of black workers,
pitched battles between young gangs of whites and blacks, interracial
violence at military bases and training camps, and some two hundred
battles between the races in forty-seven cities.

Willkie responded by redoubling his public pronouncements

against racial discrimination. Ever more outspokenly he chastised both Republicans and Democrats for their equivocation on civil rights issues. He lambasted Roosevelt for kowtowing to white supremacists in the Democratic party, and he excoriated his fellow Republicans for reneging their heritage. Urging the GOP to reclaim the legacy of Lincoln, Willkie explicitly advocated that the Republicans endorse broadened federal powers to ensure equal voting, equal employment, and equal educational rights for African Americans. Nothing less, he added, would bring blacks back to the Republican fold. "The very fact that the Republican party was the instrumentality through which the Negroes were given freedom," Willkie asserted, "makes them more resentful that it should join in acts which prevent them from obtaining the substance of freedom."[22]

Whatever his political calculations, Willkie agreed almost instantly to Walter White's request that he appear on a special coast-to-coast radio program opposing racial violence. Like most other Americans, Willkie had been shocked by the race riot in Detroit in June 1943, the worst such bloodletting in the nation's history. Detroit's riot toll included thirty-four persons killed, more than seven hundred injured, over two million dollars in property losses, and a hundred million man-hours lost in war production. For Willkie, a new day had dawned in racial affairs and the nation could not just return to business as usual. On July 21 he broadcast "An Open Letter to the American People." He had said much of it before, but never with such conviction or to so many millions of bewildered Americans.

Willkie began by surveying the scope of nationwide racial violence, emphasizing that the many instances should not be viewed as singular cases but as a profoundly dangerous national phenomenon, and an even greater threat to America's security in the world. "Two-thirds of the people who are our Allies do not have white skins. And they do have long, hurtful memories of the white man's superior attitude in his dealings with them. Today, the white man is professing friendship and a desire to cooperate and is promising opportunity in the world to come when the war is over. . . . Race riots in Detroit do not reassure them." He enumerated the civil rights to which the African American is entitled—equal protection of, and under, the law; equal opportunity of education; equal opportunity to work and the same pay for the same job; no poll tax; the right "to fight for his country in any branch of her armed services"—and insisted that "we must see to it that he gets them." Willkie again criticized both political parties for failing to secure civil rights legislation: "One party cannot go on fooling itself that it has no further obligation to the Negro citizen because Lincoln freed the slave, and the other is not entitled to power if it sanctions and practices one set of principles in Atlanta and another in Harlem." Willkie ended by relating fascism to racial prejudice: "Such an attitude within our own borders is as serious a threat to freedom as is the attack without. The desire to deprive some of our citizens of their rights . . . has the same basic motivation as actuates the Fascist mind when it seeks to dominate whole peoples and nations. It is essential that we eliminate it at home as well as abroad."[23]

In *Look* magazine several months later, Willkie termed civil rights the most important issue facing the United States. He reminded readers that "while democratic government rests on majority rule, the essence of freedom is the protection of minorities. . . . Now, above all times, we must make these principles a reality, because the whole world is watching us. Only if we can make individual liberty a reality among Americans, can we hope to gain adherents to our cause among other peoples." And, with an eye on the political campaigns to come in 1944, Willkie concluded: "We must not protect these rights fitfully, inconsistently and with political purposes, as has the present administration."[24]

Whether Willkie gained political advantage from his pronouncements on civil rights is problematic. Walter White, both to encourage Willkie to continue advocating a platform almost identical to the NAACP's and to put pressure on the Democrats to do more for civil rights, kept insisting that Willkie was cutting into FDR's popularity with African Americans and would garner a lion's share of the African-American vote against Roosevelt. At the same time an autumn poll in the *Pittsburgh Courier* indicated that nearly 85 percent of black voters favored Willkie as the next year's Republican candidate for the presidency. A quite different political message came from the pollster Elmo Roper, however, who warned that

Willkie's handling of the race issue was political dynamite and that voters would reject him for being too aggressively concerned about the plight of African Americans.[25]

Shunned by congressional Republicans and most of the GOP's local leadership, Willkie ran a distant fourth in the Wisconsin primary, the first test of his political popularity in 1944, and withdrew from the nominating race. Adding insult to injury, the Republicans then declined to invite the shaggy-haired Hoosier to address the convention, to testify before the platform committee, even to be seated as a delegate. Freed from whatever confines political ambition or party leadership had imposed, Willkie continued to espouse advanced positions on racial equality, on the need to save the Jewish people of Europe, and on the importance of safeguarding the civil liberties of all Americans.

His last political will and testament came in a series of five articles written in June to affect the party platforms, his own model platform, and two postmortems on the inadequacies of the platforms adopted by the Democrats and the Republicans, published as *An American Program* the day before he died in October. No memorial could have been more fitting. The boy from Elwood, which had a reputation among African Americans as "the home of race prejudice," the onetime symbol of big business conservatism, ended as a political prophet clamoring that racism was the crisis of American democracy. "I write," Willkie proclaimed in the first of the articles devoted wholly to the issue of civil rights, "with the deliberate intent of helping to arouse a public opinion that will require these candidates to put aside generalities, evasions and pious platitudes and deal in concise, concrete terms with this human, this national, this world problem." Like nothing before, alleged Willkie, the war has spotlighted the injustice in America's racial attitudes and actions, and "has made us conscious of the contradictions between our treatment of our Negro minority and the ideals for which we are fighting." If blacks are dying to protect liberty they must have the right to live and enjoy liberty. They "have learned that there is nothing more democratic than a bullet or a splinter of steel. They want now to see some political democracy as well." They deserve, and are entitled to, the same rights as other Americans. "The Constitution does not provide for first and second class citizens." African Americans should have an equal chance for economic advancement, an equal share of public services and funds, an equal opportunity to acquire an education of equal quality as given to other citizens, and an equal right to fight for their country in any branch of the armed services, as well as federal protection against mob violence, lynching, and state requirements that effectively disfranchise blacks.[26]

Accordingly, Willkie judged both party platforms in 1944 "tragically inadequate." He blamed the Democrats for surrendering to "the old-line 'white supremacy' bloc of Southern Democrats" and accused the liberal Dr. Jekylls of political expediency in yielding to the reactionary Mr. Hydes on the key political issue of our time. "To call the section on the Negro a plank is a misnomer," he quoted an NAACP declaration. "It is best characterized as a splinter . . . a mouse of evasion." The Republican platform was just a bit better. It specified such problems as lynching, discrimination in the armed forces, and poll taxes that prevent African Americans from voting, but instead of pledging to enact federal remedies—"which constitute the only practical method by which the Negro's rights can be assured him"—the GOP repeated "the old states rights argument and a narrow interpretation of federal power." It had "a magnificent chance to state in modern terms a code of practice that would make real the very principle of freedom upon which the party was founded." Instead, it proposed a grab bag of congressional inquiry, inadequate state law, and a time-consuming, difficult, and unnecessary constitutional amendment that combined will still fail to ensure justice to blacks.[27]

In the blunt, muscular phrases so characteristic of the hearty Willkie, he asserted, in the final words penned before he suffered a coronary thrombosis, that the "Negro lives in our midst under discriminations which differ from the racial discrimination practiced by our enemies, the Nazis, only in that ours are illegal and that we are free—if we wish—to fight against them." Restating the major theme of his racial pronouncements since the start of the war, Willkie emphasized the "repercussions all around the world that result from our treatment at home of our colored citizens. . . . We cannot be on one side abroad and the other at home." Making real the promise of democracy for African Americans "will be the test of our sincerity and of our moral leadership in the eyes of hundreds of millions all over the world."[28]

The black press mourned him as the "nation's number one patriot," the African American's "foremost champion."[29] The NAACP and several other civil rights and civil liberties organizations that had received most of the proceeds from *One World* jointly moved into better quarters in Manhattan after the war, naming it the Wendell Willkie Memorial Building. And at his gravesite in Rushville, Indiana, the granite open tablet quoting Willkie's words concludes: "We must establish beyond any doubt the equality of men."

NOTES

1. Joseph Barnes, *Wendell Willkie* (New York, 1952), 37–38, and Ellsworth Barnard, *Wendell Willkie: Fighter for Freedom* (Marquette, Mich., 1966), 66–67.

2. Bishop R. R. Wright, Jr., "No Hope for the Race in Willkie Candidacy," *Norfolk Journal and Guide*, October 26, 1940.

3. Barnes, *Wendell Willkie*, 164, and Barnard, *Wendell Willkie*, 147.

4. Wendell Willkie, "Fair Trial," *New Republic*, March 18, 1940, 370–72.

5. *New York Times*, August 28, 1940.

6. *Pittsburgh Courier*, July 4 and Oct. 12, 1940.

7. *New York Times*, November 12, 1940.

8. Clayton R. Koppes and Gregory D. Black, *Hollywood Goes to War* (New York, 1987), 18, 42–45, 86–87.

9. *New York Times*, September 14, 1941.

10. Samuel Walker, *In Defense of American Liberties* (New York, 1990), 136.

11. Barnes, *Wendell Willkie*, 321.

12. Carol King, "The Willkie I Knew," *New Masses*, October 24, 1944, 10–11.

13. Barnes, *Wendell Willkie*, 323–24, and *United States v. Schneiderman*, 320 U.S. 118 (1943).

14. *New York Times*, January 29 and June 14, 1942.

15. Wendell Willkie, "Address to National Conference of Christians and Jews," February 7, 1942, Speeches Material, Wendell Willkie Papers, Library of Congress, Washington, D.C.

16. Wendell Willkie, "The Case for the Minorities," *Saturday Evening Post*, June 27, 1942, 14 ff.

17. Steve Neal, *Dark Horse: A Biography of Wendell Willkie* (Garden City, N.Y., 1984), 272; Barnes, *Wendell Willkie*, 326–27; and *Baltimore Afro-American*, April 15, 1942.

18. Wendell Willkie, "Address at Freedom House," March 19, 1942, Speeches Material, Willkie Papers, Library of Congress.

19. Walter White, *A Man Called White* (New York, 1948), 199–202; *Pittsburgh Courier*, August 8, 1942; and Barnard, *Wendell Willkie*, 338.

20. Wendell Willkie, "Address to National Association for the Advancement of Colored People," July 19, 1942, Speeches Material, Willkie Papers, Library of Congress.

21. Wendell Willkie, *One World* (New York, 1943), esp. 14–19, 91, 181–82.

22. Neal, *Dark Horse*, 274.

23. Wendell Willkie, "An Open Letter to the American People," July 21, 1943, Speeches Material, Willkie Papers, Library of Congress.

24. Interview in *Look*, October 5, 1943. Also see Wendell Willkie, "Address to National Association for the Advancement of Colored People," May 26, 1944, Speeches Material, Willkie Papers, Library of Congress.

25. Neal, *Dark Horse*, 276.

26. Wendell Willkie, *An American Program* (New York, 1944), 7–8, 48–49, 58. Also see Wendell Willkie, "Citizens of Negro Blood," *Collier's*, October 7, 1944, 11ff.

27. Willkie, *An American Program*, 5–8, 33, 39, 58.

28. Ibid., 48–49.

29. *Chicago Defender*, October 14, 1944, and *Pittsburgh Courier*, October 14, 1944.

Indiana University debate team, 1916. Willkie is in first row, center. Lilly Library, Indiana University, Bloomington.

David E. Lilienthal of TVA presents Willkie, president of Commonwealth and Southern, a check for purchase of Tennessee Electric Power Company. Indiana State Library, Indianapolis.

Willkie talking crops in Rushville, Indiana, 1940. Lilly Library, Indiana University, Bloomington.

Willkie, the new Republican presidential nominee, June 1940. Lilly Library, Indiana University, Bloomington.

Willkie's arrival in Elwood, Indiana, August 1940. Edith Willkie is seated to his right, son Phillip in the right front seat. Lilly Library, Indiana University, Bloomington.

Willkie's acceptance speech, Elwood, August 1940. Lilly Library, Indiana University, Bloomington.

A pose of Republican unity for the 1940 campaign. Left to right, Robert A. Taft, Willkie, and Arthur H. Vandenberg. Lilly Library, Indiana University, Bloomington.

Willkie campaign parade, Los Angeles, September 1940. Lilly Library, Indiana University, Bloomington.

Willkie campaign speech on the Circle, Indianapolis, October 1940. Indiana State Library.

Willkie and King George VI during Willkie's trip to war-torn Britain, early 1941. Lilly Library, Indiana University, Bloomington.

Willkie, actress Joan Bennett, and NAACP head Walter White, July 1942. Special Collections, University Library, University of California, Los Angeles.

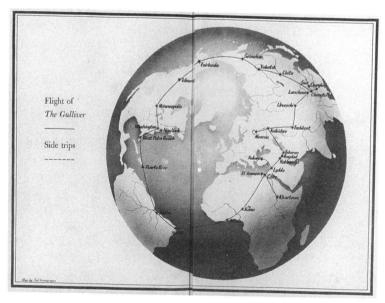

Route of Willkie's plane, *The Gulliver*, around the world in fifty days, August–October 1942, reproduced from Willkie's *One World* (1943). Lilly Library, Indiana University, Bloomington.

The Gulliver and travelers of *One World*. Indiana State Library.

Willkie with General Bernard Montgomery at the North Africa front, September 1942. Indiana State Library.

Charles de Gaulle on Willkie's right, Beirut 1942. Lilly Library, Indiana University, Bloomington.

On the street in Baghdad, 1942. Lilly Library, Indiana University,
Bloomington.

Nightmares in some quarters, 1943. Lilly Library, Indiana University, Bloomington.

PART II

Wendell Willkie
&
the World

HOWARD JONES

One World

AN AMERICAN PERSPECTIVE

WENDELL WILLKIE had more influence on causing the American people and government to turn away from isolationism in the years from 1940 to 1944 than anyone other than President Franklin D. Roosevelt. And yet Willkie, who had converted from the Democratic party a scant year earlier, held no official position except as the Republican nominee for president in 1940. A liberal in a conservative party, he could only be a maverick, an outsider to Republican stalwarts such as Herbert Hoover, Robert Taft, and Arthur Vandenberg. Overcoming this opposition, Willkie demonstrated his sincerity, outstanding speaking ability, and unquestioned character to attract the support of tens of thousands of Americans, along with that of numerous leading newspapers and magazines. His pronouncements on domestic concerns are well-documented, but few writers have brought sufficient focus to his ideas relating to foreign policy. Willkie was, according to his chief biographer, the personification of America's virtues in fighting against great odds for great causes that crossed national borders.[1]

Willkie's main objective was to convince Americans to join a world peace organization and thereby promote equality among all peoples, regardless of race, color, or nationality. As part of this global vision he urged Americans to recognize the interdependence of domestic and foreign policy, especially on the matter of civil rights at home and the country's affairs abroad. World War II was a struggle for freedom, he insisted, and not only for the present but for the aftermath of peace. A new universal order based on self-determination must replace the archaic ideas of colonialism, isolationism, and racism. All peoples must participate in and benefit from the new system. "Only the strong can be free," Willkie proclaimed, "and only the productive can be strong."[2]

Thus the central issue in Willkie's entire political life was the ongoing conflict in America between internationalism and isolationism. An avid advocate of Wilsonian ideas, Willkie urged Americans to accept a worldwide peace organization and thereby avoid their predecessors' tragic mistake during the interwar period. "The League of Nations," he wrote a friend in 1942, "was the religion of my young life." Willkie had always opposed war. In high school he called for America's participation in world affairs. As a soldier in World War I, he fought for Wilson's democratic precepts, only to see them founder in the period afterward. As a lawyer in Ohio during the 1920s he became a principal figure in the American Legion, and as a speaker at numerous patriotic gatherings, he fervently called for the nation's involvement in international affairs. Before a Rotary Club gathering in July 1925 he made a plea for the maintenance of peace: "I do not care whether peace comes through leagues, courts, international agreements or otherwise. I only ask that the children of today be so educated to the futility of war that peace will come in the next generation." Willkie declared that the crucial difference between him and the isolationists was that they did not believe that the democratic world was interdependent. They were wrong. The United States could not isolate itself from the world. It bore heavy moral, political, and economic responsibilities to other peoples. *"The world cannot get along without the United States of America,"* Willkie repeatedly insisted. *"What happens in the rest of the world must inevitably have profound effects on us in America."*[3]

Willkie stepped up his battle against isolationism during the late 1930s by warning Americans of the growing menace of Germany and Japan. Unlike his fellow Republicans—particularly his rivals for the party's nomination in 1940, Taft, Vandenberg, and Thomas

Dewey—Willkie argued that the Atlantic and Pacific no longer afforded free security. "In my judgment," he told a large audience in May, "a man who thinks that the results in Europe will be of no consequence to him is a blind, foolish and silly man." By the spring of that year Willkie expressed what he considered to be a widespread American feeling when he approved Roosevelt's call for safeguarding Great Britain with every means short of direct military involvement. If the Allies fell, Willkie warned so would America's sense of security likewise collapse. France and England were America's "first line of defense against Hitler." In St. Louis he attacked fellow Republicans for stubbornly holding on to isolationism and, in one of his many public statements that they bitterly denounced as heresy, remarked that Roosevelt saw, "more clearly than most men, the real threat of Hitler."[4]

The alarming chain of events in Europe contributed to Willkie's push for the nomination and gave him a public and national forum for stating his views on foreign affairs. In the April 1940 issue of *Fortune* magazine, during the aftershock of the Soviet invasion of Finland, he emphasized the importance of trade to international relations. The world today was "so closely knit, the oceans are so small, and the peoples of the world are so dependent upon each other, that it is not realistic to make domestic policies without considering their relationship to foreign affairs. . . . It makes a great deal of difference to us—politically, economically, emotionally—what kind of world exists beyond our shores." In urging public support for the administration's reciprocal trade treaties, Willkie argued that an effective American foreign policy would, "in the long run, *help to raise the standard of living of the rest of the world.*" Later, in a speech at a rally for United China Relief, of which he was a director, he more closely tied his arguments for global trade to personal freedom and the rejection of isolationism. The isolationist, he proclaimed "believes that while international trade may be desirable, it is not necessary. He believes that we can build a wall around America and that democracy can live behind that wall. He believes that America can be made self-sufficient and still retain the free way of life." But the internationalist "denies this. The internationalist declares that, to remain free, men must trade with one another—must trade freely in goods, in ideas, in customs and traditions and values of all sorts."[5] In June, France fell to the Nazis, providing further impetus to Willkie's success in securing the nomination that same month.

Even during the presidential race Willkie supported most of the administration's foreign policies as part of his overarching effort to maintain national unity. In a move that surprised many observers, he favored conscription and won the president's praise for helping break a logjam in Congress that blocked passage of the Selective Service Act until September. After a cabinet meeting in August, the president asked William Allen White, an advocate of aiding the Allies, to use his friendship with Willkie to seek his support for the hotly debated destroyer bases deal with England. Willkie reluctantly approved the idea, though not publicly. In his August speech formally accepting the Republican nomination, he tacitly lent his support by emphasizing that the British navy was integral to America's defense and trade. Britain's loss of control in the Atlantic, he explained, would permit Germany's domination of that great ocean as well as its control over European ships and shipbuilding. The United States would have to engage in a massive naval and air defense buildup along the Atlantic Coast. When Roosevelt resorted to an executive agreement to secure the destroyer bases deal, he was accused by many Americans of resorting to dictatorial methods. Willkie at first only noted that the president "did not deem it necessary in connection with this proposal to secure the approval of Congress or permit public discussion prior to adoption." Two days later, however, Willkie turned to the attack: "Now, leaving out of account the advantage or disadvantage of the trade, the method by which that trade was effected was the most arbitrary and dictatorial action ever taken by any President in the history of the United States."[6]

Willkie stepped up his criticisms of the administration when Roosevelt called for all assistance to the Allies short of war while, according to his opponents, hypocritically promising to maintain peace. At one point in the rising fever of the race, Willkie left the implication that Roosevelt had made secret assurances of assistance to England and was not truthful in proclaiming his interest in peace. Indeed, on October 30 Willkie warned that if Roosevelt were reelected, "you may expect we will be at war." This charge angered the president. Before a large crowd of mainly Irish Americans in Boston, he played to their desire to stay out of the war and to their hatred for England. "And while I am talking to you mothers and fathers," Roosevelt dramatically declared, "I give you one more assurance. I have said this before, but I shall say it again and again and again: Your boys are not going to be sent into any foreign wars." The Democratic platform had included at the end of this statement the words, "except in case of attack," and when someone mentioned this to Roosevelt, he crisply replied: "Of course we'll fight if we're attacked. If somebody attacks us, then it isn't a foreign war, is it?" Willkie was infuriated with Roosevelt's duplicity. "That hypocritical son of a bitch!" he roared afterward. "This is going to beat me!"[7] A week later Roosevelt won reelection by five million popular votes.

After the campaign, however, Willkie focused exclusively on the nation's welfare in continuing his support for the president's foreign policy, particularly that part of it calling for the highly controversial lend-lease bill. Roosevelt had requested Willkie's assistance in securing passage of the measure, which would authorize the manufacture or procurement of "any defense article for the government of any country whose defense the President deems vital to the defense of the United States." Willkie had not planned to comment publicly on lend-lease until he realized that isolationists in the Republican party who were attacking the measure would lose the battle and in so doing would effectively bar the party from office in coming elections. To a friend he explained that "when Hoover, [Alfred] Landon, Dewey, Taft, and Vandenberg all came out in a frontal assault on the Lend-Lease Bill, I thought I owed a duty to speak for it." The problem, he explained, was not just "to keep America out of war, but to keep war out of America."[8]

As part of his fight for lend-lease, Willkie received Roosevelt's permission to make a trip to beleaguered England in February 1941—a trip that captured the public imagination on both sides of the Atlantic. While bitter Republicans blasted Willkie as the president's man, Willkie declared that his aims were pure and simple: to collect information about England's needs and to see firsthand how badly the nation had been hurt by German air assaults. Roosevelt supported the visit because, he told Secretary of Labor Frances Perkins, Willkie could bring unity to the war effort. "For a long time," she later wrote, "it had been clear in Roosevelt's mind that our foreign policy, with the possibility that we might have to enter the war, must be not the province of our party or of a President, but the conviction of both parties and their leaders. Roosevelt knew that Willkie's trip would help toward unity."[9] In a letter of introduction prepared for Willkie's meeting with Prime Minister Winston Churchill, the president praised his emissary for keeping politics out of international affairs.

In England Willkie aroused nationwide interest and support. He met many dignitaries, including Churchill, King George VI and Queen Elizabeth, Foreign Minister Anthony Eden, and Labor Minister Ernest Bevin. Willkie also toured the docks and homes of London and other places heavily damaged by bombs, and there, surrounded by the press, he conversed with large numbers of citizens and publicly praised their courage and resilience. The visit was an immense boost to British morale. A writer from the Associated Press wrote Willkie three years afterward: "I often to this day hear British people say that you certainly did give them a badly needed shot in the arm just at the time they needed it most." As for Willkie, his support for the British intensified as he related their plight to universal principles. To the English gathered in heavily bombed Coventry he declared that "in the face of totalitarian attack, free men feel a common brotherhood."[10]

Willkie returned to the United States even more determined to see Congress pass the lend-lease bill. At the public hearings of the Senate Foreign Relations Committee on February 11, he testified in the packed chamber that Americans had to renounce isolationism and help the British resist German aggression. Lend-lease would not guarantee against United States involvement in the war, he allowed, but it presented the best possibility of staying out while providing another barrier to totalitarian control. Indeed, Willkie now showed that lend-lease had greater possibilities than the immediate objective of winning the war. Americans "must lay the moral, intellectual and spiritual foundations for the kind of world we want our children to inherit. That world . . . must be a world in which

America will share with other nations the responsibilities—and the great prospects—of peace."[11]

The bill encountered fierce though expected opposition from leading Republicans on the committee—Hiram Johnson, Arthur Capper, Gerald P. Nye, and Vandenberg—who repeatedly reminded Willkie of his accusations during the recent presidential campaign that Roosevelt was purposefully taking the United States into the war. Willkie bent his huge frame forward into the microphone, but then, as if he realized the fruitlessness of attempting to make a rational explanation in the midst of a bitter and politically inspired attack, he simply declared: "Again I protest. I struggled as hard as I could to beat Franklin Roosevelt, and I tried to keep from pulling any of my punches. He was elected President. He is my President now." The thousand plus spectators broke out in applause, causing the chairman to rap the meeting to order and to warn that he would clear the room if such an outburst occurred again. Senator Nye then returned to the attack by quoting one of Willkie's campaign charges that if Roosevelt were reelected he would have the United States in the war by April 1941. Willkie drew laughter by remarking that if he said that "it was a bit of campaign oratory," then wittily declared: "I am very glad you read my speeches, because the President said he did not." At the renewed burst of laughter Nye dropped the matter.[12]

Opponents of the lend-lease bill failed. By nearly a two-to-one margin it won the committee's acceptance the day after Willkie's testimony. On March 8 the Senate approved the bill by the same margin, and three days later the House of Representatives concurred. That same day, March 11, President Roosevelt signed the measure into law.

Willkie deserves considerable credit for the Lend-Lease Act. Roosevelt thought so. His speechwriter, Robert Sherwood, later recorded: "Once I heard [Harry] Hopkins make some slurring remark about Willkie and Roosevelt slapped him with as sharp a reproof as I ever heard him utter. He said, 'Don't ever say anything like that around here again. Don't even *think* it. You of all people ought to know that we might not have had Lend Lease or Selective Service or a lot of other things if it hadn't been for Wendell Willkie. He was a godsend to this country when we needed him most.' " Secretary of State Cordell Hull's top assistant, Carlton Savage, was even more generous with praise: "There's no question that Willkie was the real hero."[13]

During the spring of 1941 President Roosevelt considered sending Willkie to Japan to emphasize America's hardening feelings about recent world problems, then on to China, Singapore, Australia, and the Dutch East Indies to demonstrate Western unity against Japan. But in December, before the trip could take place, the Japanese attacked Pearl Harbor and catapulted the United States into the war.

America's involvement in World War II afforded Willkie the opportunity to broaden his perspective on global affairs by expressing his revulsion for extreme nationalism, which, he believed, led to discrimination in both racial and commercial practices. Out of isolationism, he warned, grew "narrow, nationalistic views" that caused racism and thereby endangered democracy. "Race antagonism is but one of the symptoms—narrow nationalism is the fundamental cause." The United States must use World War II not only to destroy tyranny but also to advance world peace and order. The United States was primarily to blame for the democracies' failure during the interwar period to establish a permanent peace. It rejected the League of Nations and the World Court, and it hurt the international economic system by passing inordinately high tariffs. The United States must change its world view and act on the axiom that "he who wins wars must maintain the peace."[14]

Thus, as Willkie saw things, his prime objective of securing American participation in the establishment of an international peace organization necessitated the guarantee of civil liberties to all peoples, including the world's nonwhites. The war made clear the wrongs of racism, inside and outside the United States. Having read the writings of sociologist Gunnar Myrdal, Willkie was convinced that the war was critical to blacks and that the racial issue was the central problem in a democracy. Indeed, racial equality was the center point of America's relationship with the world. At a meeting of the Republican National Committee on April 20, 1942, Willkie declared: "It has long been the proclaimed policy of the Republican party that a community of people cannot exist half slave, half free. The progress of human events, of science and technology, of communication and of political and economic institutions, has been such . . . that it is no longer realistic to limit this enduring principle to the shores of any single nation, however large." In Los Angeles three months later he declared: "Democracy is what we are fighting for—so let's have it here." Even though Willkie did not launch a direct attack on U.S. "relocation centers" for Japanese Americans during the war, he did so indirectly when he denounced war itself as a cause of intolerance. At the invitation of the *Saturday Evening Post*, Willkie published an article arguing that the "threat to racial and religious, even to political, minority groups springs in wartime from two things: an overzealous mass insistence upon general conformity to majority standards, and the revival under emotional strains of age-old racial and religious distrusts."[15] Americans must replace these outmoded canons with a more progressive program for the world.

World War II, Willkie declared, offered a unique opportunity to advance the cause of freedom. Americans had three choices afterward: "narrow isolationism, which inevitably means the loss of our own liberty; international imperialism, which means the sacrifice of some other nation's liberty; or the creation of a world in which there shall be an equality of opportunity for every race and every nation." In actuality, he insisted, Americans had no choice because freedom was indivisible. The "idea of equality," he explained, contains "the only sure hope of the future. . . . Let us keep that aim shining before us like a light—a light for the people of Europe, for the people of Africa, for the people of Asia, for the people of South America, and for the people of our own beloved land."[16] Americans could not keep freedom to themselves. If they wanted freedom, they had to share it with others.

Willkie also became a leader in understanding the vital relationship between the nation's racial policies and its need to maintain allies in the postwar era. Before several thousand gathered at the annual meeting of the NAACP in Los Angeles in July 1942 he emphasized the common aims of mankind in denouncing "race imperialism." White Americans' feelings toward blacks exemplified this evil. "When we talk of freedom and opportunity for all nations the mocking paradoxes of our own society become so clear they can no longer be ignored. . . . Today it is becoming increasingly apparent to thoughtful Americans that we cannot fight the forces and ideas of imperialism abroad and maintain a form of imperialism at home." A year later, in the immediate aftermath of the Detroit race riots of June 1943, Willkie declared over radio that America's racial attitudes had international as well as domestic repercussions. "Two thirds of the people who are allied with us do not have white skins. . . . Today the white man is professing friendship and a desire to cooperate and is promising opportunity in the world to come when the war is over." Nonwhites now wonder, "When the necessities of the war cease to make cooperation valuable to the white man, will his promise mean anything?" Recent race riots in Detroit, Los Angeles, and Beaumont, Texas, were not reassuring.[17]

The high point of Willkie's push for one world came in 1942, when in August he departed on what turned out to be a forty-nine-day trip around the globe as a special envoy of the president. Crossing the equator twice, he logged thirty-one thousand miles in a grueling but enormously satisfying journey that solidified his views on foreign affairs. Although Willkie later explained that he had wanted to demonstrate national unity in winning the war, "accomplish certain things for the President," and explore how the Allies could win the war, he also sought evidence to substantiate his call for one world.[18] In a four-engined army bomber and accompanied by Gardner Cowles, publisher of *Look,* and Joseph Barnes, former overseas correspondent for the *New York Herald Tribune* (both then with the Office of War Information), Willkie visited Africa (in the dangerous period immediately following the battle of El Alamein), the Middle East, the Soviet Union, and China. Of the areas he saw, the Middle East most affected his already strong detestation of colonialism and stratified societies. Unless the West adopted a new policy toward these peoples, he prophetically warned, they would follow fanatic leaders and cause the former colonial powers either to withdraw in humiliation or resort to the use of force in an ill-advised effort to stay.

Willkie's world tour did not take place without exposing hard feelings both at home and abroad. It alienated many of the Republican faithful who had supported him in 1940 and who now wanted him to remain in the country and campaign for their election in 1942. Willkie was not happy about being unable to visit India, which was then pushing for independence from Britain and, for the sake of wartime Allied unity, had to remain closed—particularly in light of his known views on Western colonialism. In Chungking, Nationalist leader Chiang Kai-shek expressed bitterness with the Allies, especially England, for what he considered to be inadequate supplies and discriminatory treatment. Willkie responded by attacking the Allies for not making a full effort to help China and by arranging for Madame Chiang to visit the United States. Then, during a meeting in Moscow with Soviet Premier Joseph Stalin, Willkie tried to smooth over the Russians' anger regarding the recent British decision (which grew out of the needs of the coming North African campaign) to divert ships carrying American lend-lease goods away from Murmansk and to Scotland instead.

But the biggest furor came when Willkie entered the ongoing controversy between the Anglo-American allies and the Russians regarding the opening of a second front in Western Europe. In Moscow, he characteristically ignored the war's political and military realities by publicly calling for an immediate second front that might relieve the Russians of the full brunt of the German offensive: "Personally," he declared, "I am now convinced that we can best help by establishing a real second front in Western Europe at the earliest possible moment our military leaders will approve. And perhaps some of them will need some public prodding. Next summer might be too late." Willkie, it became embarrassingly clear, had not been briefed about the imminent Allied invasion of North Africa; nor did he realize that the necessary men and materiel were not yet available to launch a second front in Western Europe. Further, his indiscreet comments about the need for "public prodding" infuriated both American and British military leaders. When Roosevelt expressed displeasure with the controversy arising from this impolitic statement, Willkie bitingly responded from Chungking that "when I speak for myself, I'm Wendell Willkie, and say what I damn please."[19]

The final phase of the tour, in China, further convinced Willkie of the importance of eliminating colonialism throughout the world. Looking at orphaned children in Chungking, he movingly declared that they "challenge us to answer the question, Are we fighting this war to re-establish a world under which these children lost their parents, or are we fighting to eliminate imperialistic spheres of influence, mandates and the like, which only sow the seeds of future wars?" World War II was "a war for men's minds." The West must win the support of "nearly three-fourths of the people of the world who live in South America, Africa, Eastern Europe and Asia." This did not mean that they had to accept democracy. But the West must realize that they were "determined to work out their own destiny under governments selected by themselves." It must help them "train governments of their own choosing," and it must make "ironclad guarantees administered by all the United Nations jointly that they shall not slip back into colonial status." The war must end "the empire of nations over other nations." The West must make this promise now, "not after the war." In a radio broadcast to the Chinese people, he proclaimed that "the old colonial days are past."[20]

Willkie's task was not easy, for he was asking the West to reverse a centuries-old imperial policy. The veteran New York Times correspondent Anne O'Hare McCormick wrote that his reaction to the fruits of colonialism was that of "the sensitive and open-minded American who sees for the first time a strange, awakening world."[21] Though Willkie's ideas were not new, they had never come so forthrightly from a person in such high public position and in a period of such global strain. Roosevelt, of course, had issued public declarations against colonialism, but when pressed by his British ally he ultimately retreated from what had only appeared to be a major departure from the past. When, in Chungking, Willkie pronounced colonialism dead, the president criticized his emissary's failure to consider the British side of the issue.

Willkie, however, did not relax his anticolonialism. In his meeting with Roosevelt upon returning to the United States in October, Willkie warned that the Middle East was a potential caldron of trouble and emphasized that the region looked to the West more for ideas than for material aid. Indeed, Nazi doctrines had found large-scale acceptance among peoples desperately seeking an alternative to Western colonialism. "This is not a pleasant report to make," he told the president, "but the traditions of British rule in the Middle East have created a vacuum as far as the Arab peoples are concerned, a vacuum which we have not filled and which the Germans and Italians are in part filling through our default." The United States must oppose "an indefinite perpetuation of British imperialism in this area." It must instead call for "the establishment of political freedom and economic liberty."[22]

In Willkie's "Report to the People," which all four major radio networks carried to perhaps thirty-six million listeners, he urged Americans to think on a global scale and to realize that common goals of comfort and security held all peoples together. The time was propitious, he insisted. Hatred of imperialism was strong against Western Europe and not the United States. But the goodwill toward Americans was fast dissipating because of their failure to make war aims clear. Many outside the United States wanted to know if the Atlantic Charter's call for self-determination applied to nonwhites. Thus military conquest was not enough, Willkie warned. "We must win the peace."[23]

To achieve this objective, Willkie called for liberal education throughout the world. "Freedom is of the mind" and thus the fount of all other freedoms, he proclaimed at Duke University in January 1943. At Union College in New York late that same year, he declared that "the final victory will be won on the battlefields of men's minds."[24] Such a goal was admittedly difficult to achieve during a burgeoning age of technology, but the freedom of the individual must take priority. People were people, regardless of nationality, race, and color. They shared the same needs and desires, and they all had an inherent equality as human beings. The United States must therefore condemn isolationism because its proponents lacked this essential belief in universalism. It must condemn imperialism because such a doctrine led to colonialism. It must condemn totalitarianism and great-power domination of the world. Above all, it must refuse support to antidemocratic regimes while helping former colonies make the transition to independence.

Willkie's ideas attracted worldwide attention, for in April 1943 he published them in a short book that touched the popular pulse and became an instant best-seller. By the first of August *One World* had sold 1,550,000 copies. It remained first on the *New York Times Book Review* best-seller list from May through early September. By October 1944 the book had been translated into nearly every foreign language; nearly three million copies had been printed and distributed, including those that made their way via the underground into Nazi-occupied countries in Europe. The prestigious journal *Foreign Affairs* praised Willkie's attack on isolationism, and *Commonweal* lauded his "moving appeal for self-government among the peoples of the Far and Middle East, for the end of white imperialism everywhere, and for the immediate creation of international machinery that will learn to keep the peace by helping to win the war."[25]

Willkie's book was enormously popular because it expressed the sentiments of millions of people throughout the world. Willkie called for a "council today of the United Nations—a common council in which all plan together, . . . a council of grand military strategy on which all nations that are bearing the brunt of the fighting are represented." His main argument was that "nothing of importance can be won in peace which has not already been won in the war itself." While the war was still going on, the United Nations must develop the organization by which they could maintain the alliance for freedom into the postwar period. Otherwise the war's efforts would be "moving from one expediency to another, sowing the seeds of future discontents—racial, religious, political—not alone among the peoples we seek to free, but even among the United Nations themselves."[26]

The only way to peace, Willkie added during an Independence Day broadcast in 1944, was to proclaim "a declaration of interdependence among the nations of this one world."[27] Even though many of Willkie's ideas aroused Roosevelt's support at one time or another, they were out of touch with world politics of the moment. The British (and the French) could not approve all these principles without permanently discarding what was left of their prewar empires.

The views espoused by Willkie also failed to attract the support of "revisionist" or "new Left" writers, who criticized "one worldism" as arrogant, dangerous, and self-interested. Rather than using free trade and foreign assistance to promote the general welfare of the international community, they argued, Washington's policy-makers had fallen under the influence of Wilsonian idealists and big business in establishing a self-righteous and exploitative "open door policy" that sought to spread democracy by engaging in ideological crusades and to enhance America's economic and political power by searching out and controlling overseas markets and raw materials. Although the revisionists had trouble in demonstrating a direct connection between business and the making of foreign policy, they raised serious questions about an approach that could lead to global intervention and conflict. Further, they insisted, America's effort to establish world order could lead to repression of legitimate indigenous upheavals on the basis of their alleged leftist thrust.

Admittedly, Willkie's one world views had the potential to bring about these problems, but the evidence does not show that he envisioned a program aimed at preventing world revolution by restoring the conservative capitalist order. Based on both his private and public statements, he believed it vital to world peace to provide everyone with the economic and social essentials of life in order to establish a global community based on fundamental democratic freedoms.

After an unsuccessful bid for the Republican nomination for the presidency in 1944, Willkie resumed his call for one world. In his brief work published that same year, *An American Program,* he summarized what he thought were the greatest problems facing the country at the time of the election. He had wanted the Republicans (and the Democrats) to adopt these ideas in their platforms. But he soon realized at his party's convention in Chicago that his effort was a failure. Economic ties among nations, he nonetheless declared, were the key to peace. But these same nations also had to guarantee safety to minorities. In both domestic and foreign circles the United States would be measured by its acceptance of an international role and by its treatment of racial groups. Foreign and domestic policies were inseparable: "What happens in either immediately affects the other."[28]

Treatment of blacks in the United States, Willkie reiterated, would have an important impact on the nation's foreign policy. Blacks realized that their anguish was part of the global struggle for freedom. Indeed, Willkie proclaimed, fairness to blacks at home would be "the test of our sincerity and of our moral leadership in the eyes of hundreds of millions all over the world." The war had revealed glaring contradictions between U.S. attitudes toward blacks and the ideals for which the war was being fought. He could not emphasize enough that "in the world today whatever we do *at home* affects our foreign policy, and whatever we do *abroad* affects our foreign policy." The two issues were inseparable. "On no single question is this truth so inescapable as in the repercussions all around the world that result from our treatment at home of our colored citizens." There was a "growing determination among colonial, subject and minority peoples everywhere" to win universal freedom. "We, as Americans, cannot be on one side abroad and the other at home. We cannot expect small nations and men of other races and colors to credit the good faith of our professed purposes and to join us in international collaboration for future peace if we continue to practice an ugly discrimination at home against our own minorities, the largest of which is our thirteen million Negro citizens."[29]

Willkie also again emphasized the importance of free trade to the spread of democracy. The United States must gradually revise the tariff downward and work toward a worldwide stabilization of currency. Reciprocal trade agreements were crucial in the effort to end "economic imperialism." In a statement that portended a major feature of American foreign policy after the war, he urged the government in Washington to "take the initiative in new reciprocal agreements of a multilateral nature so that trade will begin to flow again." Financial investments were acceptable in undeveloped countries, but Americans must also extend technological assistance. Everyone would profit from the higher standard of living resulting from wider economic gains in the world. "The chief need of the transition period will be relief, rehabilitation and the liquidation of foreign owned balances—in other words, the problem is how to carry lend-lease to its logical conclusion."[30]

Willkie's life was cut short by a heart attack a month before the 1944 election. This was "shocking news," Sherwood wrote later.

Willkie "had served a great purpose in times of direst peril." Indeed, Sherwood reminisced, had Willkie gotten the nomination, Roosevelt might not have chosen to run again. "I had no tangible basis for this belief," Sherwood admitted, "and it was a doubly hypothetical surmise because it was evident for a long time to Roosevelt that Willkie had no chance whatever of being nominated. Greatly as the Old Guard lords of the Republican machine hated Roosevelt, they had come to hate Willkie even more, and, be it said to his eternal credit, Willkie went out of his way to court their hatred by scorning their support."[31] Willkie's objectives, Sherwood noted, were so close to those of Roosevelt's, and the president had so much respect for his longtime friendly adversary, that he would have been willing to see the executive office pass into Willkie's hands. As an indication of this feeling, during the summer of 1944 Roosevelt had privately authorized an approach to Willkie about establishing a new political coalition based on liberal principles that would cross party lines and concentrate on winning both the war and the peace. But the letter from Roosevelt calling for such a discussion somehow made its way to the press, and Willkie, for political reasons, had to keep his distance from Roosevelt. In mid-September, however, after Willkie had lost the nomination to Dewey, he seemed to lean toward the reelection of Roosevelt by urging independents to vote for the candidate most in favor of an international peace organization.

The vehement opposition of the Republican conservatives, the special relationship Willkie had with Roosevelt, the consistency of Willkie's arguments throughout his life—all suggest that his liberal stand in foreign affairs was sincere. During a vacation at his home in Rushville, Indiana, he presented a convincing case to liberal writer Samuel Grafton of the *New York Post*. In the living room of his farmhouse, Willkie explained the philosophy underpinning *One World:* "I tell you that if a man is not, deep in his belly, in favor of the closest possible relations with Britain and Russia, then it does not matter what else he is. This is the touchstone to a man's entire position in politics today. Only occasionally does it happen that one issue arises which is so controlling that every other issue is subsidiary to it, and this is it." With Grafton's attention riveted on his host, Willkie continued his emotional plea for one worldism. It was "not enough," he declared, "for a man merely to repeat the right words about world collaboration. He has to be on fire with it. He has to feel, in his belly, that this is the door which will open outward to an expansion of American activity and prosperity. You cannot be wrong on this issue and right on any other." In an article entitled "I'd Rather Be Right," Grafton wrote afterward that Willkie had "two fixed poles" in his political life: "an interest in civil liberties and an interest in international collaboration."[32]

Although correct in noting the main points of Willkie's philosophy, Grafton did not go far enough in recognizing the relationship between the poles themselves. Willkie realized that civil liberties and international cooperation were inseparable: America's treatment of its minorities at home was vital in determining how much influence the nation would wield in the world at large. During the late 1940s and afterward, when the United States emphasized containment in stopping the spread of communism into the Third World as well as other parts of the globe, the various presidential administrations in Washington grasped the importance of dealing with nonwhite peoples on an equal basis. Such a policy became especially troublesome to implement, however, when white Americans bitterly refused equal treatment to their own nonwhite fellow citizens at home. One worldism was not merely a collaboration among nations, Willkie years earlier had proclaimed; it was collaboration among peoples that crossed national, ethnic, and racial lines.

Like Woodrow Wilson, Wendell Willkie has undergone intense criticism for advocating a vastly expanded role for the United States in international affairs. But also like Wilson, Willkie was not afraid to declare that the United States must regain the "moral leadership of the world." And, like Wilson, Willkie argued that the United States must be willing to give up some rights and privileges to reach an agreement conducive to international goodwill. Otherwise any international organization would be only "a consultative pact" of "peace-loving" nations. As Wilson had lamented more than two decades before, Willkie expressed deep concern about the ultranationalists in the United States who opposed any organization that would *"limit the sovereign right of all nations to make war at will."* By cooperating with other nations in this manner, Willkie insisted, the United States would be "using, not sacrificing, America's sovereignty to the end for which it was intended: the security and peace of the American people." Americans must abandon their "traditional definitions of sovereignty" and their "exaggerated respect for the two thirds rule."[33]

What were Willkie's contributions? It might be an overstatement to conclude that his efforts were crucial in persuading Americans to think beyond their national borders and to support their nation's involvement in the United Nations. It might also be an exaggeration to argue that his challenges were vital to the demise of Western colonialism and to the agonizingly slow realization in the United States that racial matters could not be confined to domestic affairs. It might even be stretching the point to say that his battle against the Old Guard isolationists within the Republican party contributed to a less conservative turn in leadership that permitted the nomination and election of Dwight D. Eisenhower in 1952 and thereby enhanced America's involvement in world affairs. But it would be fair to say that Willkie's declarations encouraged both political parties to accept a global foreign policy. In a country that was struggling with the dilemma of whether to look forward and accept new global challenges or to turn backward to isolationism and ignore the vast global responsibilities that came with power, he found countless adherents, and he had many other adherents in the rest of the world as well.

More so than William Jennings Bryan at an earlier time, Willkie brought real meaning to the term *loyal opposition*. Rather than bitterly assail the president either before or after the election of 1940, Willkie supported a foreign policy that he thought had the best interests of the nation at stake. A bipartisan and global approach was vital to the spread of freedom, he recognized. Isolationism rested on ideas that permitted the United States to evade the global responsibilities of fighting racism and colonialism. Before most Americans, Willkie understood the interrelatedness of domestic and foreign policy, and he knew that United States security was irrevocably intertwined with the security of the globe. Recognizing that sometimes it was good when a person's reach extended beyond his grasp, Willkie called for the implementation of universal principles, regardless of the repercussions.

The ultimate damnation of Willkie's efforts, of course, came from his own political party, and this resulted in no small measure from the warm accord he developed with Roosevelt. According to Sherwood, the president respected Willkie's "enormous courage, if not his political acumen, and was profoundly and eternally grateful for Willkie's persistent battle against the isolationism of the Old Guard in the Republican party."[34] If these same Republicans could not agree with Roosevelt's enthusiastic praise of Willkie, they most certainly would have to acknowledge that in foreign affairs he had outmaneuvered them and helped push the party away from isolationism. In so doing, Willkie helped to build a bipartisan base for this country's deepening global involvement in the perilous years following World War II.

NOTES

1. Ellsworth Barnard, *Wendell Willkie: Fighter for Freedom* (Marquette, Mich., 1966), 2.
2. Quoted in ibid., 207.
3. Willkie to Daniel Willard (the friend), May 27, 1941, cited in ibid., 326; speech before Rotary Club, ibid., 62; quote on United States, ibid., 297.
4. May speech quoted in William L. Langer and S. Everett Gleason, *The Challenge to Isolation: The World Crisis of 1937–1940 and American Foreign Policy*, vol. 2 (New York, 1952), 486; Willkie's quotes on Hitler in Steve Neal, *Dark Horse: A Biography of Wendell Willkie* (Garden City, N.Y., 1984), 75.
5. "We, the People, a Foundation for a Political Platform for Recovery," *Fortune*, April 1940, 171, 173; speech before United China Relief rally in Neal, *Dark Horse*, 209.
6. Willkie's defense of President Roosevelt in *New York Times*, September 4, 1940, 1; his attack, ibid., September 7, 1940, 8.
7. Willkie's October 30 quote in Robert A. Divine, *The Reluctant Bel-*

ligerent: American Entry into World War II, 2d ed. (New York, 1979), 105; Roosevelt quote in Robert E. Sherwood, *Roosevelt and Hopkins: An Intimate History* (New York, 1948), 191; Willkie's response to Roosevelt's speech in Barnard, *Willkie,* 258.

8. Lend-lease bill quote in *New York Times,* January 11, 1941, 3; Willkie to Robert P. Allen (friend), January 17, 1941, cited in Barnard, *Willkie,* 275; Willkie quote on keeping America out of war in Neal, *Dark Horse,* 187.

9. Frances Perkins, *The Roosevelt I Knew* (New York, 1946), 118.

10. AP writer Eddy Gilmore quoted in Barnard, *Willkie,* 284; Willkie's Coventry quote in *Daily Herald* (London), February 3, 1941, 6, cited in ibid., 284.

11. Quote in ibid., 287.

12. Quotes in James MacGregor Burns, *Roosevelt: The Soldier of Freedom, 1940–1945* (New York, 1970), 48–49.

13. Quotes by Sherwood and Roosevelt in Sherwood, *Roosevelt and Hopkins,* 635; Savage quoted in Neal, *Dark Horse,* 206.

14. Willkie's quote on nationalism in telegram to Maxwell Anderson, July 29, 1944, cited in Barnard, *Willkie,* 303; Willkie's quote on wars in "Let's Look Ahead," *New York Times Magazine,* February 15, 1942, 33.

15. Willkie's quote before Republicans in Barnard, *Willkie,* 328; Willkie's Los Angeles quote in *New York Times,* July 19, 1942, 10; Willkie, "The Case for the Minorities," *Saturday Evening Post,* June 27, 1942, 14.

16. Quote on America's choices in *New York Times,* May 12, 1942, 13; quote on equality, ibid., April 24, 1942, 5.

17. Willkie's quotes before NAACP, ibid., July 20, 1942, 28; Willkie, "Postscript" to CBS radio broadcast, "Open Letter to the American People," ibid., July 25, 1943, 25.

18. Quote in Barnard, *Willkie,* 347.

19. Quote on second front in *New York Times,* September 27, 1942, 3; Chungking quote, ibid., October 8, 1942, 3.

20. Chungking quote, ibid., October 5, 1942, 3; quotes about end of colonialism in Neal, *Dark Horse,* 251; quote on colonial days in *New York Times,* October 7, 1942, 10.

21. McCormick quote in Barnard, *Willkie,* 372.

22. Willkie's statements to Roosevelt highlighted in Willkie's "Draft notes for conversation with President Roosevelt. October 14, 1942," cited in ibid., 375–76.

23. Quote in *New York Times,* October 27, 1942, 8.

24. Duke quote, ibid., January 15, 1943, 13; Union College quote, ibid., October 14, 1943, 5.

25. *Commonweal* quote in Neal, *Dark Horse,* 264–65.

26. Wendell L. Willkie, *One World* (New York, 1943), 165, 178, 179.

27. Willkie's Independence Day quote in Barnard, *Willkie,* 418.

28. Wendell L. Willkie, *An American Program* (New York, 1944), 22.

29. Ibid., 7–8, 48–49.

30. Ibid., 21, 24, 46.

31. Sherwood, *Roosevelt and Hopkins*, 830–31.

32. Willkie's quotes in Neal, *Dark Horse*, 283; Grafton article in *New York Post*, October 16, 1944, cited in Neal, *Dark Horse*, 283.

33. Willkie, *An American Program*, 25, 41–42, 44.

34. Sherwood, *Roosevelt and Hopkins*, 635.

ANDRÉ KASPI

One World

A VIEW FROM FRANCE

LET ME BEGIN with a confession. Until a short time ago I had never read Wendell Willkie's *One World*. No French translation of the work is available, it is impossible to find an English-language version in French bookstores, and it requires much patience and not a little luck to succeed in borrowing a copy from any of our major libraries. Willkie the unknown—and not only to me. A random survey in France today doubtlessly would reveal that the French are unaware that Willkie wrote and published a book that sold over a million copies—or, for that matter, that he ever existed.

That is not surprising. As Willkie was attaining notoriety in the United States and as Americans were looking to him with interest, many with enthusiasm, France was living through the terrible summer of 1940. The armistice with Nazi Germany had been signed on June 22, with Fascist Italy on June 24. Marshal Pétain was the final head of government of the Third Republic. On July 10 he was voted the full powers that allowed him to found the French State. This French State was a sort of repentant France, devastated by its defeat,

This essay was translated by Barbara Brady Pieroni. Numbers in parentheses refer to page numbers in Wendell L. Willkie, *One World* (New York, 1943).

plagued with remorse for having created the Popular Front, constantly preoccupied with the fate of its million and a half prisoners of war, and already persuaded that England would not be able to withstand the assault of the Luftwaffe. France was divided in two by the demarcation line: to the south, Pétain's kingdom with its center in Vichy; to the north, the occupied zone with a Paris delivered into the hands of the victors, plastered over with signs and banners in German, submitting to Hitler and his henchmen. It goes without saying that the presidential campaign in the United States went unnoticed. The French had neither the time nor the inclination to learn more about the Republican candidate. At best they listened distractedly to what was being said in a country which, it was recalled, had fought against the Germans in 1917–1918 and from whom France had waited in vain for help during the dark days of June 1940.

At the same time—and this did nothing to spark an interest in Willkie among the French—President Franklin Roosevelt was finishing his second term in office and had put in his bid for a third. Roosevelt had been a very familiar name since 1933 and even before. His New Deal had set off much debate in the prewar French press. Was his the formula that would lead the United States out of the Depression? Was it a strong enough response to the Fascist agenda? Could France draw inspiration from Roosevelt's policies? To a certain extent Léon Blum's government had been sensitive to the winds of change in America. In 1936–1937, there had been exchanges back and forth across the Atlantic. As for the effects of United States foreign policy, it had surprised the French when Roosevelt torpedoed the London Economic Conference of 1933; it had irritated them when the wave of isolationism swept across the New World; it had created hope, and even illusion, when the president of the United States, in the days following the Munich Conference, raised the possibility of political quarantine for the aggressors and initiated a tentative rapprochement with the European democracies. In short, everyone knew Roosevelt; many admired him. Paul Reynaud, Marshal Pétain's immediate predecessor as premier, had expected miracles from Roosevelt and had received only kind words of encouragement. Roosevelt moved among the greats. That was not the case with Willkie.

Furthermore, in the race to the White House, the loser is always left in the shadows. He will never reap the rewards of celebrity; foreigners will never know his name. Such was the sad fate not only of Willkie but also of Landon, Dewey, Stevenson, McGovern, and others. Nixon was spared this fate only because his battle with Kennedy was broadcast on television and because the defeated candidate of 1960 was the victor in 1968 and 1972.

And yet the French would probably have been interested in the career of a man like Willkie. The businessman who was a latecomer to politics, the Democrat who broke with Roosevelt's party to become the Republican candidate, the adversary of a president with whom he had so many ideas in common, the natural leader who generated powerful support: these ingredients would have transformed Willkie into an international media star, had the media been in 1940 what it has become since, and had France been in a curious mood. Circumstances denied the encounter between this extraordinary man and the rest of the world.

Other circumstances, however, gave Willkie the opportunity to take center stage. In 1942 Roosevelt selected him as envoy for a special mission abroad. This decision may seem surprising in that Roosevelt was a Democratic leader calling upon the aid of a Republican, but it is easily explained by the fact that the war had created a holy bond. Moreover, Roosevelt had already appointed two Republicans to positions in his government in 1940, in a symbolic gesture of national unity. Willkie left the United States on August 26, 1942, and returned forty-nine days later, having like Phileas Fogg gained a day by crossing the international dateline from west to east. He had covered thirty-one thousand miles. It is true that Willkie was already back in the States when the Anglo-American forces landed in North Africa. This landing marked the first time in the history of World War II that the Americans had succeeded in taking hold in Algeria and Morocco, that is, in territories under French control. But Willkie had met with Montgomery in El Alamein, spent time in the Near and Middle East, visited Stalin in the

Kremlin, traveled in the Yakutsk Republic, reached China, and engaged in long conversation with Chiang Kai-shek and the members of his entourage. Quite an itinerary! Thus Willkie had been able to observe firsthand the state of the globe, to follow closely the unfolding of military operations, to discuss political evolution and the plans that would shape the postwar world. He returned to Roosevelt with impressions, information, and ideas that would prove to be of primary importance in the shaping of American diplomacy.

In Willkie's *One World* the reader discovers a talented journalist who is precise in his descriptions. Willkie speaks warmly of several people he had interviewed: Montgomery, Stalin, Chiang—to name only the best known. He writes in a language that is pleasant to read. Some passages are marked with a literary flair. It is easy to understand why the work was an immediate success. Willkie not only gives an account of his trip but also uncovers the complexity of the world to his fellow countrymen in his simple and direct style. He doesn't pretend to be an expert who has already seen it all, understood every move, anticipated every outcome. Willkie's eyes are opened in wonder. His mind remains alert and receptive as he attempts to grasp intellectual currents and to better understand his hosts. In this sense his readers have no trouble identifying with him. He sounds like an average American who is becoming aware of the enormity of the problems and the complexity of the solutions. At the same time he serves always as a guide, taking the hands of his readers, the somewhat disoriented Americans who are ill at ease about their country's new role.

All the same, one discovers certain surprising gaps in the itinerary of the pilgrim from the White House, even when difficulties presented by the military situation are taken into account. Willkie did not go to the Maghreb, and we know that the events unfolding there at the time were to be of crucial importance for what was to come. He never set foot in Europe, at least if we are willing to concede that Moscow is not quite in Europe. Yet he would have had no trouble getting to England in late 1942. (He had been there in early 1941.) He could have met in London with representatives of the governments in exile of Norway, Denmark, Poland, and Free France and discussed the future of Europe with them. He made stops in

Turkey, Egypt, Palestine, Iran, and Iraq. He reflected at length on the future of this region of the world during his stays in Cairo, Beirut, Baghdad, Tehran, and Jerusalem. But he did not go to India, still a British colony, perhaps because the divergent policies of London and Washington made such a stop impossible and because his visit might have been misinterpreted by the British government. This was an important omission in his itinerary and one that the Asian representatives whom he visited did not fail to underscore, returning often to the subject of India's future. It seems that Willkie was not unaware that this was an omission. As for Indonesia, the Philippines, and the immense Pacific, Willkie could not possibly have taken the pulse of these regions while the battle was raging: that whole theatre of operations was inaccessible to all outside civilians, even should they be personal representatives of the president of the United States.

All in all, one does not tire of following Willkie through those seven weeks. Quite the opposite. Both yesterday's reader and today's can learn much about the time and the man, about the war and the United States. And one question keeps coming to mind. Does this very successful book, quickly devoured by the Americans in 1943, lead us inevitably to certain conclusions as we read it in the last decade of the twentieth century? Was it at least a herald of the postwar world? Had Wendell Willkie understood the changes that were taking shape and prepared his fellow Americans for what was to come after the war?

The answer would appear to be no. Intentionally or not, Willkie closes his eyes and ears to problems which now seem essential to us. To a Frenchman, for example, the question of France's future. Willkie mentions France on several occassions. He discusses its relative size, he notes that the country is under Nazi domination and has been reduced to slavery. As he is writing his account, he reflects on the 1942 deal negotiated between General Eisenhower and Admiral Darlan, the second in command in the Vichy government, a deal ratified by President Roosevelt on the grounds of "temporary military expediency." Willkie refutes the Eisenhower-Roosevelt argument that the Americans would have suffered heavy losses had they landed in North Africa and refused to enter into an agreement with Darlan. He reports that the people whom he interviewed in the Near East had questioned him about Washington's pro-Vichy policy and had not failed to register amazement. The reader is anxious to reach the account of his meeting with General de Gaulle.

This account is disappointing. The two men meet in Beirut. Willkie is greeted at the airport with a reception worthy of the heyday of the French Empire. There are colonial troops and a military band. De Gaulle welcomes him in a palace crawling with saluting guards; the general's office is filled with busts, statues, and portraits of Napoleon. They begin a conversation that continues late into the night. De Gaulle talks like some kind of a mystic. "I cannot sacrifice or compromise my principles," he says in reference to the French mandate on Syria and the Lebanon. One of the members of his entourage adds, "Like Joan of Arc" (23). That is a meaningful reference in 1943. In January of that year, when de Gaulle and Roosevelt had finally met in Casablanca, the general had evoked France's great saviors Joan of Arc and Clemenceau, after which Roosevelt, who loved to tell a good story, real or invented, had spread the word around that de Gaulle took himself for Joan of Arc. Willkie conveys the same idea. The image he gives us of the man of destiny is blurred by passion, resentment, and irony. From this point of view, Willkie is very Rooseveltian; a good many other of his fellow Americans could not help but be moved by the glory of de Gaulle's epic struggle. Willkie is less Rooseveltian when he expresses his interest in the Fighting French movement. De Gaulle cuts him short and corrects him; the Fighting French are not a movement but the rightful "legatees" of France and its possessions. De Gaulle, according to de Gaulle, represents France and the glory of its history. Until the French on French soil have recovered their political freedom, the relinquishment of the mandate on Syria and the Lebanon is out of the question.

Once again we expect Willkie to draw fresh conclusions about French resistance and about de Gaulle's inflexible will to assume the full responsibility for governing of a conquered and occupied country. But he does no such thing. Willkie limits his comments to a reflection on the future of the French mandate and concludes his analysis by citing the remarks of a high government official who, when asked whether he would prefer that the mandate be held by the English or the French, replied, "A plague on both their houses" (24). Willkie does add that he believes the French must not go back into Indochina. As for the rest, silence. One has to wonder whether the former Republican candidate was being careful not to embarrass Roosevelt, whether he really had nothing to say about the relations between Washington and Vichy from July 1940 to November 1942 or about France's future after the war and the possibility of its status as a major power, in short, whether his vision of France differed from that of his Democratic adversary of 1940.

Willkie disappoints us again in his treatment of the war itself. Since he had not been to Europe, he does not even recall for his readers the origins of the conflict. Now and again he mentions the misdeeds of Nazi Germany, but he never gives a concrete example of the crimes that had been and were still being committed by Hitler and those under his command. This attitude can be illustrated by two examples. The reader is expecting Willkie to explain why the war had taken on the character it had, that it was a war of ideology, unlike the other wars the world had been fighting for centuries before it. Willkie remains incredibly discreet on the question of Nazism, its intellectual content, its social and political repercussions, the subjection of man and of a part of the European continent in which it resulted.

This is not to say that the author of *One World* can be charged with the slightest complacency. His plea for freedom and democracy is so forceful as to prove any such accusation unfounded. "If we want to see the opposite of this American system," he writes, "we have merely to look at the military despotism of Hitler and the autocracy of Japan, and the fading dictatorship of Fascist Italy. The story of Germany for the last ten years has been one of racial and religious intolerance that provided a mask behind which a peace-professing dictator lured the people first to minority persecution, then to war" (194). Nonetheless, his analysis remains superficial and consequently does not prepare his readers for a thorough understanding of what the postwar era will bring. It may be, however—and only this would justify the silence Willkie maintains—that for him the condemnation of Nazism is a given, that he assumes all

Americans have well understood what Hitlerism represents and that it is no longer necessary to explain it to them.

There is another regrettable omission: it was in the late summer and early fall of 1942 that precise accounts of disturbing dimensions began to replace what had until then been only rumors of a Jewish genocide. Both Washington and London had been informed by Gehrart Riegner, the representative of the Jewish World Congress in Geneva, as early as August 8. The State Department received confirmation in the weeks that followed. In November daily newspapers in the United States were publishing articles. The Nazis had killed by tens of thousands the Jews living in the Soviet territories invaded by the Wehrmacht. They had perfected industrial methods for killing in the extermination camps; in Auschwitz and Birkenau the gas chambers were operating at full force. Willkie makes no comment. Is this because he was skeptical about the validity of the reports, which many could not bring themselves to believe? Was it his position that fighting "the war of the Jews" was not the principal objective of the war? And yet, at the time of his visit to Jerusalem he had fully understood the complexity of the Palestinian problem, the all but insurmountable difficulty of satisfying both the Zionist Jews and the Arab nationalists. Henrietta Szold, an American woman who had played a part in the founding of Hadassah, had spoken to him about "the persecuted Jews of Europe," about the necessity of an understanding between Jews and Arabs, and about the goodwill of the Zionist leaders. Had Willkie given his readers some details about the persecution he might have awakened them to the urgency of the question and to the true nature of the war.

A third and final disappointment: Willkie offers no plan for the Europe of tomorrow. He forcefully demonstrates that if the victory of the Allies in 1918 had not brought peace to the world, it was because this victory had not been founded on new principles, because it had allowed nationalisms and imperialisms to survive and thereby had necessarily provoked frustration and exasperation. Which is to say that when the Second World War has come to an end, new systems and principles must be put to work. Which ones? What sort of territorial divisions should then be considered? Will it be absolutely necessary to modify the borders of 1939 or 1937?

Will Germany remain a single state or will it be divided? Will a con-
federation of West European states be formed? Will the future of
Europe itself be a casualty of the war? Will its role in vital decision-
making be taken over by the United States or the Soviet Union?

There are so many issues on which we would like to have heard
Wendell Willkie's views. He only goes so far as to recommend the
recreation of the smaller countries of Europe into independent political units, on the condition that they not be created as separate
economic and military entities. We have to admit that this is a rather
vague statement of principles. Willkie maintains his prudent reserve,
either because he had not set foot in Europe or because he had no
precise ideas to propose. Whatever the reason, the reader's expectations are frustrated.

On the other hand, to three of the issues discussed in his work
Willkie brings certain insights whose timeliness has not been lost
almost a half century later. The first of these concerns the position
the United States must take toward the rest of the world. Isolationism is, he tells us, dead and gone. That is no revelation in 1942–
1943, for the Republican candidate of 1940 had spoken in similar
terms. This time Willkie makes an effort to reinforce his position—
which is also that of Roosevelt—by relating what had been told him
in the course of his trip and what he had been able to deduce from
the attitudes of the people he had encountered. From the Middle
East to Russia, from Turkey to China, there is everywhere an enormous "reservoir of good will" available to the United States: "I found
that they all have one common bond, and that is their deep friendship for the United States" (158). In the Middle East, British imperialism is still very much alive, and there remains a French
imperialist presence. In spite of foreign criticism directed against its
frequently racist behavior, the United States remains one of the
world's greatest hopes. Stalin admires American efficiency and has
high expectations for the effects of U.S. aid. The Chinese, led by
Chiang Kai-shek, are solid supporters of friendship with the United
States. Had Willkie been able to visit India, he would no doubt have
found many more friends of his country. What were the reasons for
this widespread enthusiasm? First, the United States was present
throughout the world, represented by its doctors, its teachers, its

engineers, its cinema, and its economic system; and second, this presence was seen to be a disinterested one.

What this means is that the Americans have a role to play, and what a role! The outcome of the war and the success of peace truly depend on them: "No other Western nation has such a reservoir. Ours must be used to unify the peoples of the earth in the human quest for freedom and justice" (161). This determines the responsibilities of the United States in defining the goals of the war. Willkie recommends the formation of a council of United Nations that would make both military and economic decisions and would define the policies to be followed concerning the defeated and conquered countries. If not, "we will find ourselves moving from one expediency to another, sowing the seeds of future discontents—racial, religious, political—not alone among the peoples we seek to free, but even among the United Nations themselves" (179).

It is in this sense that there is now only one world. Advances in transportation prove it. The extension of the conflict confirms it. The prospect of a secure peace demands it. If the United States were to give in to the old demon of isolationism, the planet would once again become a place full of danger for all of its inhabitants. Willkie's conclusion is as valid today as it was in 1943: "America must choose one of three courses after this war: narrow nationalism, which inevitably means the ultimate loss of our own liberty; international imperialism, which means the sacrifice of some other nation's liberty; or the creation of a world in which there shall be an equality of opportunity for every race and every nation" (202).

Should the United States send aid to the Soviet Union and collaborate with its government? To Willkie the answer is clear. It is in the interest of the United States to fight side by side with the Soviets against a common enemy. Not a moment's hesitation. One of his chapters is entitled "Our Ally, Russia." The second chapter devoted to the Soviet Union, more precisely to the Republic of Yakutsk, ends with this appeal for cooperation: "I believe it is possible for Russia and America, perhaps the most powerful countries in the world, to work together for the economic welfare and the peace of the world" (102). He has said it all in a few words. The possibility of a Cold War had not even occurred to him. In his enthusiasm

Willkie forgets all caution, in spite of the fact that he openly concedes to his readers that he spent only two weeks in this fascinating and mysterious country. One of Willkie's appeals for cooperation between the United States and the Soviet Union strikes a common chord in a generation of Americans. The Soviet Union is beginning to look more and more like the United States. Flying over Russia and its vast stretches of land, who could help but think of Texas? Looking down on the irrigated valley adjoining Tashkent, one is reminded of southern California. Bordering the length of the Volga there is a collective farm of eight thousand acres which supports fifty-five families; that is about 140 acres per family, just like in Rush County, Indiana. Willkie is invited to dinner by the manager of a kolkhoz and is charmed by the warm hospitality: "The food was abundant, simple but good, and the wife of the manager, who had cooked the meal, urged me to eat as I have been urged many times in Indiana farmhouses" (73). These are only a few examples among many. It will not be long before the two giants begin to evolve in the same direction; inevitably they will meet.

Another of Willkie's arguments makes reference to the past which the Russians have miraculously survived. Their economy had fallen behind. Their society had scarcely known progress. It was not until the Revolution of 1917 that modernization had begun to take hold. Many of their methods are being borrowed from the Americans, who for this reason carry part of the responsibility for the continuation of this evolution. Finally, the war has served only to reinforce the spirit of patriotism. It must be that Soviet society is a strong society; it will hold together in spite of the blow delivered it by the war against Germany. At the head of this immense empire is Stalin, a simple and straightforward man, ready to laugh at a joke, who is well-informed on the international situation. Stalin's plans for the postwar world are perfectly acceptable. The Americans have nothing and no one to fear: "No, we do not need to fear Russia. We need to learn to work with her against our common enemy, Hitler. We need to learn to work with her in the world after the war. For Russia is a dynamic country, a vital new society, a force that cannot be bypassed in any future world" (87).

Once again Willkie gives little or no analysis of the content of Stalin's ideology. He wasn't shown its negative aspects. Perhaps he had some suspicions, for during his visit to Yakutsk a Polish woman whispered in his ear certain details about the Soviet system that ran counter to the offical propaganda. Nor does he fail to remind his reader that, to many, Yakutsk is known as "the people's prison." How would he have reacted when the Western world learned of the existence of the Gulag? How would he have interpreted the split between the superpowers in 1946 and the bipolarization that divided the planet into two blocs from 1947 to the end of the 1980s? The fact remains, however, that Willkie raised a question that has still not been resolved, and may not be for a long time to come. Should the United States and more generally speaking the countries of the West attempt to transform the society and the economy of the Soviet Union by working closely with its leaders, making investments, and exporting some of their technology? Or should they rather demand social and economic change, more political freedom, and more free market economy before making a gesture toward Moscow? No one would deny that these questions are still pertinent today.

Willkie devotes a quarter of his book to China, which attests to the importance he grants it. He seems more at ease in this part of his work than in the others. His writing reveals a certain fascination with China that is shared by many Americans, a sense of responsibility on the part of the United States, and the idea that it is in the Far East that the possibility of lasting peace will truly be determined. To a certain extent Willkie and Roosevelt are of one mind. China has already become one of the Big Four. In conformance with the principles outlined by the Atlantic Charter and the Four Freedoms, Westerners, in this case the British and the Americans, will no longer be the masters of that part of the globe. Once Japan has been defeated, China, which is not seeking to build an empire, which possesses immense resources, and which is much greater in size and population than the United States, will rightly reclaim Asian independence. As Napoleon said, China will awaken and the world had better take heed. Beginning, of course, with the United States.

As with the Soviet Union, Willkie continues to draw the comparison between the United States and China. A new China will undergo the rapid expansion that had characterized the American West. A modern China will develop economically just as the United States did, and probably more quickly. Along with its human resources, which are at once infinite and inexhaustible, China has at its disposal a capital whose proportions are difficult to estimate with any precision. Under the command of their leaders, the Chinese are fighting with vigor against the Japanese. Chiang Kai-shek, the Generalissimo, is a careful and thoughtful listener. He is sincere, dignified, and imperturbable. He identifies with the Chinese people; he takes time to read the Bible and to pray every day, without fail. With the help of the Americans, who have finally come to understand that the Chinese struggle is also their struggle, Chiang will bring about the recognition of China as a world power.

Willkie met also with Chou En-lai, a leader of the Communist party. He found him to be a man of great ability, restraint, and sincerity. Chou would like to see greater and more rapid reform. He is not certain that once the war and the national unity brought about by the war have ended, there will not be battle between the Communists and Chiang's Kuomintang. Is civil war then on the horizon? Willkie entertains the possibility but apparently does not lend it much credence, no doubt because of his absolute confidence in the talents of Chiang. Once again America's task is made clear: to extend friendship to the Chinese, to send over the Himalayas, through Burma or by other routes, the machines, airplanes, ammunition, and raw materials for which they have the greatest need.

A triangular diplomacy is thus taking shape. The United States, the Soviet Union, and China are the partners. Great Britain will not long resist the movement that is bringing the fall of the colonial empires. France and the Netherlands are no longer major powers. Ideology plays only a minor role, especially when that ideology is communism. Democratic principles and the thirst for freedom are too strong and attractive to be threatened.

The scope and the impact of Willkie's work must be neither over- nor underestimated. Willkie cannot be seen as a visionary who, long before his contemporaries, would have grasped the full import of the evolution taking place in his world. Nor does he hold for today's readers the necessary key to an understanding of the upheaval in our world. But he did indeed recognize the metamorphoses of his times: the advancement of the United States to the rank of super-power, the decisive role of the Soviet Union and China, the di-minished strength and position of Europe, and the insoluble complexity and explosive nature of the situation in the Middle East. It is a pity that Willkie never exercised the powers of the executive office. He had the intelligence, the lucidity, the education, and the culture necessary to play a major role. The proof lies in his book.

A. S. MANYKIN

Modernizing the Republican Foreign Policy Agenda

DURING THE 1930s AND 1940s several talented political leaders advocated various responses to the challenges facing the American nation. All gave way to Franklin D. Roosevelt and his New Deal. For most ordinary Soviet as well as American people the history of the United States during these years is virtually synonymous with the leadership and personality of FDR. Such popular belief is not completely unfounded: Roosevelt indeed played a significant role.[1] Yet the vast changes that took place in these years were not wholly outcomes of the policies of the president and his associates. Rather, a wide spectrum of opinions, interests, and demands caused change, as is characteristic of the American pluralist society. Roosevelt was fortunate in having several outstanding opponents who contributed to the restructuring of the American system, helping the nation adapt to new socioeconomic realities and to a changing international system.

Wendell Willkie was one of the most colorful personalities among Roosevelt's opponents. Although Willkie's role in American history

This essay was translated by Bhavna Dave.

is eclipsed by the formidable figure of Roosevelt, there are valid grounds to include him among those leaders most actively involved in shaping political traditions and the institution of party politics. Committing himself to the fate of the Republican party in 1939, Willkie worked toward the formation of a new Republican ideological and political credo. In the midst of intense party conflict Willkie expressed unequivocal opinions on issues of grave significance to the future of the United States. Although he entered the debate over serious domestic concerns, his most fruitful and constructive contribution came in the foreign policy sphere. Here he made a major contribution toward propagating internationalist ideas among Republicans particularly and in raising general awareness of the new role of the United States in the postwar international system. It is these aspects of his multifaceted activities that this essay seeks to illuminate, while at the same time acquainting American readers with the debates on these issues in the Soviet Union.

United States foreign policy during the interwar period was dictated by the precepts of isolationism. There is an ongoing debate among Soviet and United States historians about the meaning of isolationism, its correspondence with American national interests, and its impact in facilitating an international system.[2] It is indisputable, however, that Hitler's rise to power led to a rapid deterioration in the international situation in the 1930s as the probability of a new global conflict increased daily. Only a collective action on the part of great powers could stop the Nazis, who had never sought to camouflage their aggressive intents. Unfortunately, collective action never took place. Isolationism, which renounced the idea of collective action, proved to be a major obstacle to the creation of a system of collective security. One can wholeheartedly agree with the historian Robert Divine that "American isolation had become the handmaiden of European appeasement."[3] While the great powers were still debating a response to the aggressive actions of the Axis powers, the situation worsened in the Far East and Europe. The treacherous attack on Poland by Hitler's Germany on September 1, 1939, marked the beginning of the Second World War.

Although war began thousands of miles from the American shores, the scale of the conflict was too great to leave the United

States unaffected. Roosevelt was forced to take measures to strengthen America's defense and to provide moral and political support to the victims of Nazi aggression. The influential isolationist bloc fiercely resisted the president's drift from neutrality. Isolationists in Congress and out did not believe that the sharp turn of distant events required the United States to step forward and assume a role of leadership in the Western community of nations. Roosevelt nonetheless did his best to prepare the nation for this new role, even as his second and, according to precedent, last term as president was running out. All of these factors made the presidential campaign of 1940 decisive in determining the future of the country.[4] It was into this fiery caldron that Wendell Willkie plunged when he decided to enter the race.

Born into a middle-class family, Willkie worked his way up to become president of the giant utility corporation Commonwealth and Southern. A registered Democrat since 1912, he became dissatisfied with FDR's domestic policies and crossed over to the Republican camp. In May 1940 he published in *Fortune* magazine an article called "We the People" in which for the first time he popularized his political opinions. Willkie's originality (especially for traditional Republicanism) in analyzing a series of key questions attracted the attention of various political commentators. Though this article was primarily concerned with domestic issues, Willkie asserted also that the nation needed new formulations in foreign policy. Soon his was a common name in the press, radio, and various social organizations. Rather than revealing his own views at once, Willkie chose to provide a very sophisticated and astute critique of Republican leadership and its inability to employ effective methods of struggle against Roosevelt.[5]

It is true that on the basis of his early writings and speeches Willkie was hardly considered the person capable of leading an opposition party. To many of his fellow Republicans he remained an odd duck, seeking to distort the traditional values of the party. A survey conducted in early 1940 by the magazine *Current History* showed that only 2 percent of the editors of leading periodals felt that Willkie should win the Republican nomination, and practically nobody believed that his victory was possible.[6] The reason for such doubt was Republican opposition to Willkie's unorthodox approach to solving major socioeconomic problems. Domestic and international changes had led Republicans to begin to consider new approaches, but in 1940 the seeds of a new, more modern Republicanism were thinly scattered. New ideas remained incoherent.[7] In this difficult and confused political environment Willkie managed to devise an elaborate concept of consistent and logical policies. It was mainly his platform that was finally adopted by the Republicans in their campaign to unseat the ruling Democratic party.

It would be difficult to speculate on the turn the preelection rivalry would have taken or how Willkie's ideas would have developed had there not been an upheaval at the European borders in 1939. The crossing of the border to the West by Hitler's generals in spring 1940 heralded a dramatic turn as it became increasingly clear to many Americans that these events in Europe directly affected their national security. The hope that the United States could remain a spectator in such a monstrous conflict began to recede. How should the country respond to this foreign policy crisis? Was it possible to continue the past thinking that assumed the interests of the United States and the rest of the world were not correlated and events in Europe were no business of the United States? Or should the United States accept the fact that the world was becoming increasingly interdependent so that the Americans could no longer remain passive spectators to the events across the ocean? These questions were passionately discussed in the great debates on foreign policy in 1940. Willkie was one of the few leaders who realized early on that the unprecedented situation warranted a serious revision of the basic tenets of American foreign policy. Of course, like the overwhelming majority of his fellow politicians, Willkie also believed that direct American involvement in the military conflict was inexpedient and unwise. But he also denounced the idea of absolute neutrality. He realized that the question of who emerged as victor in this military conflict was no longer a matter of indifference for the future of a civilization that included the United States. It appeared to Willkie that the United States must ally itself with Britain and France.[8]

As expected, many Republicans regarded Willkie's ideas with little enthusiasm and saw the man himself as an unpromising dark horse in the presidential race. Leading the race were Thomas Dewey, Robert Taft, and Arthur Vandenberg. As the Republican convention approached, it appeared that Willkie was going to remain a nonentity. Foreign policy events caused an unexpected and momentous turn in the situation. The military catastrophes suffered by France in May and June 1940 stunned Americans. As the *Washington Post* commented, "If the Allies lose this war, it will prove to be the worst catastrophe for the United States in our whole history."[9] Willkie astutely foresaw a definite turn in the mood of the electorate and its leaders. His popularity began to swell in May 1940, and the day after France's withdrawal from the war he stood second only to Dewey among his main rivals.[10] It was not a matter of coincidence but rather, as one historian asserted, "the war in Europe which gave Willkie the edge over the other candidates."[11] Indeed, in spite of all the predictions to the contrary, Willkie won the party nomination in Philadelphia.

This victory at the convention signified only the beginning of Willkie's ascent in the political arena. The publishing magnate Henry Luce pointed out that "until the Republican Party can develop a vital philosophy and program for America's initiative and activity as a world power, it would continue to cut itself off from any useful participation in this hour of history."[12] Willkie fully agreed with Luce, but many prominent Old Guard Republicans were unwilling or unable to comprehend this truth. Required to give their grudging consent to Willkie's nomination as the Republican leader, they had no intention of surrendering their party's political agenda to this upstart.

The predicament in which Willkie found himself in 1940 was far from simple. The decentralized structure of the major American political parties encourages factional politics, so that the party leader is often required to resort to bargaining and compromise to consolidate an electoral base. Willkie's Republican rivals always had greater clout within the hierarchy than he had. Willkie did possess a wide range of contacts outside the party, however, especially with the press and the business community, which to some extent compensated for his lack of power within the party. His task of uniting various Republican factions remained challenging, nonetheless, and adversely affected the party's electoral agenda. Willkie had been able to ignore his opponents in his campaign for nomination. But now, having won the nomination and coming to personify the party, he was compelled to deal with many influential fellow party members who did not share his views.

Willkie's campaign focused on foreign policy. Seeking broad support, he assured voters that "in the foreign policy of the United States, as in its domestic policy, I would do everything to defend American democracy and I would refrain from doing anything that would injure it." Willkie reminded voters that "it is neither practical, nor desirable, to adopt a foreign [policy] program committing the United States to future action under unknown circumstances."[13] The logic of events forced him to take more explicit stands on some issues, however. He declared, for instance, that the defeat of Great Britain would be a serious blow to the national security of the United States. He openly stated that American interests were inimical to the plans of Hitler's Germany.[14] At his insistence the Republican party accepted (albeit with reservations) the suggestion to offer aid to countries engaged in warfare with the aggressive Axis powers, some sort of prototype lend-lease.[15] Although Willkie made no direct call for collective action against the aggressors, his articulation of a definite American response represented a serious departure from the precepts of neutrality upheld by isolationists.

Willkie's statements soon made him a target of fierce criticism by conservatives within his own party, who charged that he was moving in step with Roosevelt and away from neutrality. Sharpening his disagreements with Willkie, Taft proposed that the Republican party needed to work out a clearer alternative program to that of the Democrats. Without a well-defined identity, the Ohioan asserted, disastrous consequences would follow. In an interview with the *Nation* Taft took an apparent jab at Willkie when he declared "it is obvious that a party kills itself and removes any excuse for its existence when it adopts the principles of its opponents."[16] Taft, in fact, criticized Willkie's effort to forge some bipartisan consensus. The press joined the dispute. Criticizing the nominal head of the Republican party, the *Washington Times Herald* commented: "Instead of a knockout and drag-out political fight, this is getting to be a love feast. What important national or international issue do these candidates differ on, anyway?"[17] Friction among various factions of the Republican party thus aggravated the situation, giving an added dramatic twist to the presidential race and complicating the challenges Willkie faced.

Sensing the unsettled position of the new leader of the GOP, Roosevelt began in the final stages of the electoral campaign an assault on Willkie's platform, especially his foreign policy recommendations. That put Willkie in a precarious situation. Although he fully realized that the days of isolationism were long over and any support of it would lead American foreign policy into further deadlock, he was unable to openly say so. Driven by the logic of party competition, he was forced to criticize the practical steps taken by the incumbent president to strengthen America's position and prestige in the world. As the race approached its finale Willkie's behavior grew more intense and combative. Striving to increase his popularity among Republicans and laboring to provide an alternative to Roosevelt's policies, Willkie entered into conflicts with his own convictions, sliding into an obstructionist stand that obscured his internationalism.

Willkie thus failed to unite the ideological and factional divisions within the GOP in 1940. And in the competition between the two parties, the Democrats appeared more prepared to accept the burden of governing the country during the critical situation triggered by the spreading military conflagration. The electoral outcome was preordained; Roosevelt was elected president for the third time. Keeping in mind the rout by the Democratic party in 1936, Willkie accepted his party's defeat. It was owing largely to his efforts, however, that the beginning of a restructuring of the Republican ideological and political agenda was made possible.

An animated debate over the electoral results occurred in the press, in Congress, and among party activists. Willkie himself added fuel to the fire with a speech on "loyal opposition," delivered soon after the election. He sharply reprimanded his Republican colleagues for resorting to pure obstructionism. Willkie believed that the minority party must carry out a constructive dialogue with the ruling party.

Rather than working toward the failure of the majority party's program, it should cooperate in revising it. "Ours must not be an opposition against," he declared; "it must be an opposition—an opposition for a strong America, a productive America."[18] Willkie realized that the international situation was too grave to allow foreign policy and national security matters to be resolved by means of squabbles between the two parties.

This was the beginning of the emergence of a bipartisan foreign policy. Willkie considered the debate between isolationists and internationalists, which had characterized the course of foreign policy in the interwar period, a matter of the past. Now he actively championed the concept of the "American era," i.e., the global responsibility of the United States toward the progress of civilization (at least the Western version). This concept gradually emerged as a dominant foreign policy postulate. Appealing to the traditional concept of manifest destiny, he argued that America had a special mission to spread freedom and democracy through the world.[19] Of course Willkie's efforts toward restructuring the Republican foreign policy agenda would have been in vain had the war not shattered the ideological bastion of isolationism.

Great Britain found itself in a most perilous position by summer 1940. What would happen if Britain fell to Hitler? This question caused grave concern among Americans. The New York Times stated that "this is not only Britain's hour of peril. It is our own."[20] There were some faint hopes for America's strategic invulnerability in view of its geographic remoteness from the Old World, but the development of military technology soon shattered these hopes. The growing belligerency of Hitler further dispelled the myth of American invulnerability.

In view of these developments it is not surprising that the United States increased aid to Britain. Roosevelt sought ways for the country to remain formally a noncombatant observer and yet in fact be a noncombatant ally. Lend-lease was his primary vehicle. Introduced in Congress in January 1941, it signified an important landmark in the transition toward a new foreign policy program that affirmed the role of the United States as the leader of the Western community of nations. There is no doubt today that lend-lease was one of the most successful innovations in American diplomacy. During the debate in Congress, however, this bill was the target of the harshest criticisms. The isolationists maintained, not without valid grounds, that passing this bill would severely enhance the probability of the United States being dragged into the war. Much depended on the stand taken by Republicans. Willkie offered full support to the administration, using whatever pull he had to convince even a small part of his party to support this bill. He managed to increase his prestige as the party leader at the same time. Despite the fact that right-wing Republicans increased their demands, there was some progress in modernizing the foreign policy agenda of the party. Arthur Vandenberg, an active opponent of the internationalist course at the time, rightly noted at the passage of the lend-lease bill that "we have taken the first step upon a course from which we can never hereafter retreat."[21]

Throughout the summer and fall of 1941 foreign policy issues remained the focus of intense struggle between the two parties, as well as within them. As the United States began to depart gradually from the fundamental tenets of neutrality there remained strong opposition to involvement in the war. The attack on Pearl Harbor changed the situation dramatically. The bankruptcy of isolationism was obvious now, even to its faithful supporters such as Vandenberg.[22] Having long been a critic of the isolationist credo, Willkie found himself back in the game. Now he was able to express his views on isolationism without restraint. To Roosevelt he declared, "I am hopeful that all traces of isolationism can be washed out of both the Republican and Democratic party."[23]

On the basis of this favorable situation, Willkie ventured to expound the new role of the United States in the postwar international system. He often instructed his colleagues, "We must learn to face without flinching the great responsibilities which destiny has imposed upon us."[24] He realized that as long as modernizing the Republican foreign policy agenda was confined only to its elites it was doomed to fail. It was essential to spread these ideas among the party rank and file. Willkie was by and large successful in executing this task, aided immensely, of course, by the Japanese attack on Pearl Harbor. According to a survey conducted by Republicans immediately after the United States entry into the war, Willkie had out-stripped his nearest rival and doubled his popularity. Respondents to this survey were party activists at the county level, where isolationism had traditionally had strong roots. By 1942 the National Farmers' Union, an organization of several thousand small farmers and traditionally a bulwark of isolationism, supported the resolution "There's No Return To Isolationism." Such sentiments echoed Willkie's views that the United States must play an active role in the postwar construction of the world.[25]

Willkie's isolationist opponents were unprepared to lay down their arms, however. Having recovered from the initial shock of Pearl Harbor, they capitalized on the failure of U.S. troops in the Pacific as argument to rehabilitate isolationism, at least partially. Theirs was a direct challenge to President Roosevelt as well as to Willkie. Willkie accepted the challenge from within the party. An April 1942 gathering of the Republican National Committee in Chicago, a bastion of isolationism, generated fierce debate on how best to oppose the Democrats. Willkie's internationalist arguments carried the day when the gathering approved a resolution that was based purely on internationalist principles.[26] Despite the limited role played by the committee in intraparty affairs, Willkie's achievement was outstanding, reflecting the progress in the foreign policy thinking of his party. Similar progress was evident also in congressional debates, which showed that more and more Republican congressmen and senators were beginning to share Willkie's image of the postwar world and the role of the United States in it.[27]

Willkie's success in modifying his party's ideology by no means implied that Republicans were ready to entrust to him leadership of the 1944 campaign. The factional struggle within the party was still very much alive. Willkie realized that he must resort to other means to increase his popularity and ensure his success. One such step was a trip around the world that Willkie undertook in 1942. Planned with the support of Roosevelt to demonstrate the strength of the foreign policy consensus in the United States, the trip was intended also to display to the Republican electorate Willkie's statesmanship and grasp of international issues. This widely publicized tour undoubtedly enhanced his prestige.

Among the major stops was the Soviet Union, where Willkie met with Stalin and Molotov as well as with representatives of the Soviet intelligentsia, army, and the enterprise managers.[28] His stay was not long, only two weeks, but he had a busy schedule. No other American politician at that time had the opportunity to see various aspects of Soviet life and to meet so many people representing different social strata. It came at a very difficult period for the Soviet Union, and Willkie had to listen to numerous Soviet grievances about the alleged "go-slow" American approach to the problem of opening the second front against the Nazis in Europe. That, however, did not change Willkie's overall positive reaction to the Soviet Union and its people. He was amazed by the sincere belief displayed by the people in the inevitability of Germany's defeat and by their firm stand in defense of values on which the Soviet society of the time was based. Stalin too left a strong impression on Willkie's mind. Willkie called him "a hard man, perhaps even a cruel man, but a very able one."[29] On his return home Willkie wrote about his meetings with the Soviet leaders and the people in *One World*. The goodwill Willkie expressed toward the Soviet Union and the Soviet people was unique for a Republican and clearly singled him out from other American political leaders.

Willkie's *One World* was much more than a travel memoir about the Soviet Union. It contained reflections on his images of the postwar world and discussed how the United States must respond to the new conditions. Willkie's prescription was unequivocal: the United States must not relinquish responsibility for peacetime developments on the international front. America was destined to become the leader of the world community.[30] It is clear that the notion of the American era, so very popular in these years in the United States, had already grown strong for Willkie. This concept literally permeated his work, thought, and action. The Soviet response to the idea of an American era as Willkie and others expressed it, however, was extremely negative. Soviets saw lurking behind the notion of the American era the ideological basis of America's imperialist foreign policy ambitions and anti-Soviet bias.[31] Indeed, the expansionist element of the slogan was often emphasized within more aggressive circles of the American establishment. Of course, much depends on interpretations. We cannot know how Willkie would have fared had he been president in the postwar world. But in his discourse on the future of the United States in such a world, Willkie continued to stress the inevitability of international cooperation and the need to resolve global problems by common endeavor. The call to respect other nations existed side by side with a veiled manifestation of expansionist motives.[32] One might think that these latter ideas had outlived their times, but in reality armed force and the method of economic repression were still the predominant components in most American foreign policy thinking. The foreign policy establishment's excessive concentration on these traditional ideologies often produced extreme reactions to other nations' policies.

Willkie's *One World*, which in a few weeks sold more than one million copies, unleashed a polemic outburst of foreign policy debate, much of it in the context of disagreement within the Republican party over its position in the forthcoming presidential elections. Willkie's opponents correctly saw his increased visibility as a serious claim not only for Republican leadership but also for a final restructuring of the party's foreign policy agenda. The magnitude and speed of the radical overhaul of the party's ideology initiated by Willkie visibly frightened his opponents and stirred them to action. At the end of 1942 Joseph W. Martin resigned from his post as chairman of the Republican National Committee. Martin, who had sought to mediate in the factional struggle, was replaced by Harrison Spengler, whose first public appearances demonstrated a disposition toward the right wing. At the same time Dewey strengthened his position in the party hierarchy. The fiercest opposition to Willkie came from the Midwest. C. Nelson Sparks, the former mayor of Akron, Ohio, issued a bitterly hostile pamphlet entitled *One Man—Wendell Willkie*, announcing that Willkie had ceased to belong to the Republican party and to enjoy its mandate.[33] Another hard blow came from the Missouri Republicans, who demanded an explanation of his stand on nine questions they had prepared, questions they posed in a provocative manner designed to paint Willkie into a corner.[34] Willkie's relations with other Republicans were badly deteriorating at the same time that public opinion surveys showed a fall in his popularity.[35] At a meeting with Republican congressmen in Washington in October 1943 he openly accused them of displaying hostility toward him. Many were indeed hostile. Willkie's opponents went absolutely mad when he issued an address to American soldiers stationed abroad with a plea to vote against all congressmen sympathetic to isolationist ideas in the forthcoming elections.[36]

Interestingly, the fierce controversies over Willkie's leadership did not necessarily imply attacks on his foreign policy. This is evident in the case of Dewey. Although his relations with Willkie worsened steadily from summer 1942 on, Dewey was careful publicly to express views that were consonant with Willkie's. The resolutions approved at the most important Republican party forums in 1943 were drafted in accordance with Willkie's views. Such was the case at the Mackinac Conference, attended by practically the entire Republican elite (with the exception of Willkie). Despite the diffused manner in which the most crucial resolution pertaining to foreign policy matters was drafted at Mackinac, the resolution nonetheless betrayed an international spirit: the party urged a "responsible participation by the United States in postwar cooperative organization among sovereign nations to prevent military aggression and to attain permanent peace with organized justice in a free world."[37] This resolution received a high degree of approval from many noted Republicans, including Vandenberg. One can agree with the statement of journalist Karl Keyerleber on the outcome of the conference: "isolationism is not dead, but it no longer rides herd on the old G.O.P elephant."[38] Naturally Willkie was far from quiet. He continued fighting actively to wipe out all vestiges of isolationism from the party ideology. He continued to emphasize the bankruptcy of isolationism and to argue that only a decisive transition to an internationalist position could ensure a high degree of United States efficacy in international affairs.[39]

It was not merely a matter of resolutions and rhetoric for the Republicans to base their future foreign policy strategy on the precepts of global responsibility. It was also a policy concern, as seen in the Republicans' active participation in legislative affairs. An example of this is the initiative taken by a Republican faction in the Senate for adopting the Connally-Fulbright resolution advocating the need for American support of an international organization for maintaining peace and having the right to issue sanctions. Although the Democrats were the initiators of the resolution, its approval was a result of bipartisan support. Vandenberg, the leader of the isolationist bloc only a few years back, actively participated in this debate and was instrumental in obtaining the support of many irresolute Republicans for the new foreign policy program. Senator Harold Burton, a colleague of Vandenberg, actively helped in reorienting party foreign policy objectives. Because of his persistence, the magazine *Republican,* an organ of the national party, published his article entitled "A Path to Lasting Peace." Several ideas contained in this article were later to become the basis of the Connally-Fulbright resolution.[40] Willkie's role in this important shift in Republican thinking was far from nominal. He was one of the first persons to advocate the adaptation of Republican foreign policy to the new international situation.

It is an irony of history that the Republican party, which was in many ways obliged to Willkie, did not rush to his aid during the 1944 primary campaign. Willkie lost in the primaries of Wisconsin and was out of the race. His defeat by no means implied a rejection of the principles that he espoused, however. As appropriately noted by *Time,* "the party that met at Chicago was not the party that had lost three elections to Franklin Roosevelt."[41] The "Willkie factor" had a visible impact in framing the 1944 Republican platform. In a brochure called *An American Program* Willkie proposed a party platform. A comparison between Willkie's brochure and the Republican platform shows that the foreign policy sections were almost identical. The major concern of both was the desirability of American participation in the postwar international organization.[42] At the party convention this appeal was moderated by misgivings about a United Nations transforming itself into a supragovernment.[43] Yet even those Republicans who were opposed to the infiltration of new foreign policy concepts into the party's platform were compelled to carefully conceal their nostalgia for isolationism. Characterizing the electoral atmosphere, *Time* stated: "In the 1944 election no isolationist could find comfort. The people had spoken for international cooperation."[44]

In the postwar years the vestiges of isolationism remained suppressed as globalism became the predominant factor in America's foreign policy. Willkie did not live to see peace dawn at the end of the war nor to compare his prognostication of the future system of international relations as projected in *One World* with the real situation. He died in October 1944. In all fairness, we must concede that not all of his predictions came true. But this should not surprise us. The evolution of the postwar system of international relations was too complex to be foreseen completely. Some crucial dimensions of postwar international relations (e.g., nuclear weapons) simply did not exist when *One World* was written. But by and large Willkie accurately foresaw the course of development of American foreign policy ideals and practices. As he had predicted, the United States firmly occupied the position of leader of the Western community and in many ways defined its behavior in terms of international affairs. The nation took upon itself several international obligations that significantly affected the whole dynamic of international issues. Bloc politics (though Willkie did not quite use this term) became the important component of United States foreign policy strategy, receiving solid support from both parties.

Willkie dreamt of one world. The postwar world, however, was divided into two antagonistic camps. Who is to be blamed for this? There are different responses to this question in the United States and the Soviet Union. Clearly, Soviet and American scholars are faced with providing a thorough analysis of all the nuances of the events that led to the Cold War. And today it is important that we seek ways out of conflict situations and direct our efforts to constructing truly one world in which all countries and peoples have the opportunity for freedom and progressive movement. In this context it is useful to look back and review those aspects of Willkie's ideas which a half century ago turned people's attention to one world and mutual peace.

NOTES

1. The list of articles and monographs on Franklin Roosevelt published in the Soviet Union is sizable. See, for example, N. N. Iakovlev, *Franklin Roosevelt: Chelovek i politik* [Franklin Roosevelt: The man and the politician] (Moscow, 1969); N. V. Sivachev, "Franklin Roosevelt: Prezident deistviia i politicheskii realist" [Franklin Roosevelt: A president of action and a political realist], *SShA: Ekonomika, politika, ideologiia*, 1982, no. 1, 20–33; V. O. Pechatnov, *Demokraticheskaia partiia SShA: Izbirateli i politika* [The Democratic party of the USA: Voters and politics] (Moscow, 1980); V. L. Malkov, *Franklin Roosevelt: Problemy vnutrennei politiki i diplomatii* [Franklin Roosevelt: Problems of domestic policy and diplomacy] (Moscow, 1988). For Willkie, see A. S. Manykin, "Vendell Villkii i genezis 'novogo respublikanizma' " [Wendell Willkie and the genesis of "New Republicanism"], *Amerikanskii ezhegodnik*, 1980 (Moscow, 1981).

2. The best-known works on this critical issue in Soviet historiography are E. I. Popova, *SShA: Bor'ba po voprosam vneshnei politiki/1919–1922* [USA: Conflict about foreign policy issues] (Moscow, 1966); D. G. Nadiafov, *Narod SShA: Protiv voiny i fashizma* [American people against war and fascism] (Moscow, 1969); and A. S. Manykin, *Izoliatsionizm i formirovanie Vneshnepoliticheskogo kursa SShA, 1923–1929* [Isolationism and American foreign policymaking, 1923–1929] (Moscow, 1980).

3. Robert A. Divine, *The Reluctant Belligerent: American Entry into World War II* (New York, 1965), 55.

4. Robert A. Divine, *Foreign Policy and the U.S. Presidential Elections: 1940–1948* (New York, 1974).

5. Wendell L. Willkie, *This Is Wendell Willkie* (New York, 1940), 247–49.

6. "What's Your Opinion?" *Current History*, April 1940, 46- 47.

7. For a discussion of the process of "New Republicanism" in Soviet historiography, see *The U.S. Two Party System: Past and Present* (Moscow, 1988), chaps. 12 and 13, and A. S. Manykin, *Era demokratov: Partiinaia peregruppirovka v SShA 1933–1952* [The Democratic era: Party realignment in the U.S.,1933–1952] (Moscow, 1990).

8. Willkie, *This Is Wendell Willkie*, 265.

9. *Washington Post*, May 23, 1940.

10. *The Gallup Political Almanac for 1946* (Princeton, N.J., 1946), 209–10.

11. Conrad Joyner, *The Republican Dilemma: Conservatism or Progressivism* (Tucson, 1963), 45.

12. Henry R. Luce, "The American Century," *Life*, February 17, 1941, 63.

13. Willkie, *This Is Wendell Willkie*, 264.

14. Ibid., 265.

15. Donald Bruce Johnson, ed., *National Party Platforms*, vol. 1, rev. ed. (Urbana, Ill., 1978), 390.

16. *Nation*, December 13, 1941, 612.

17. *Washington Times Herald*, September 3, 1940.

18. *New York Times*, November 13, 1940.

19. "Wendell L. Willkie's Address of October 26," *Current History*, December 1942, 342.

20. *New York Times*, August 12, 1940.

21. Arthur H. Vandenberg, Jr., ed., *The Private Papers of Senator Vandenberg* (Boston, 1952), 10.

22. Ibid., 1; *Congressional Record*, April 22, 1942, vol. 88, pt. 3, 3637.

23. Quoted in R. Ficken, "The Democratic Party and Domestic Politics during World War II" (Ph.D. dissertation, University of Washington, 1973), 17.

24. Wendell L. Willkie, "The Price of Victory at Best Will Be High," *Vital Speeches of the Day*, February 1, 1942, 242.

25. *Congressional Record*, October 26, 1943, vol. 89, pt. 7, 8739–40.

26. *New York Times*, April 22, 1942.

27. See A. S. Manykin, "Dvukhpartiinaia sistema v gody uchastiia SShA vo vtoroi mirovoi voine" [The bipartisan system during U.S. participation in the Second World War], in N. V. Sivachev, ed., *Politicheskie partii SShA v Noveishee vremia* [Political parties in the U.S. in recent times] (Moscow, 1982), 94–129.

28. For the Soviet response to Willkie's visit, see Konstantin Simonov, *Raznie dni voiny: Dnevnik pisatelia* [Various days of the war: A writer's diary] (Moscow, 1975), 173–77. Simonov, a writer of poetry and fiction, had access to Joseph Stalin and top-ranking Soviet officials of the time. His best-known work is his trilogy about World War II, *Zhivye i mertvye* [The living and the dead].

29. Wendell L. Willkie, *One World* (New York, 1943), 83; see also 53–54. Many years after Willkie's visit I met Konstantin Simonov, who described Stalin in nearly the same words used by Willkie. Willkie's impressions of his visit and Simonov's remarks about the American's stay were very similar. The main point of both was that the United States and the Soviet Union should move to more cooperation, no matter how different their respective systems of values were.

30. Ibid., 202–3.

31. See, for example, N. N. Iakovlev, ed., *SShA: Politicheskaia mysl' i istoriia* [USA: Political thought and history] (Moscow, 1976).

32. Willkie, *One World*, 177, 187, 190, and passim.

33. C. Nelson Sparks, *One Man—Wendell Willkie* (New York, 1943), 42–46.

34. *Congressional Record*, October 11, 1943, vol. 89, pt. 6, 8203.
35. *Gallup Political Almanac for 1946*, 211.
36. *New York Herald Tribune*, August 13, 1943.
37. *Congressional Record*, September 20, 1943, vol. 89, pt. 6, 7649–50.
38. Karl Keyerleber, "G. O. P.—New Blood and Old Horizons," *Current History*, November 1943, 220.
39. Wendell L. Willkie, "Our Sovereignty: Shall We Use It?" *Foreign Affairs*, April 1944, 347–61.
40. *The Republican*, March 1943.
41. "Republicans," *Time*, July 10, 1944, 17.
42. Wendell L. Willkie, *An American Program* (New York, 1944), 23; Johnson, ed., *National Party Platforms*, 407.
43. Johnson, ed., *National Party Platforms*, 407.
44. "What Happened," *Time*, November 13, 1944, 19.

ADDRESS OF WENDELL L. WILLKIE, FOUNDATION DAY,

Indiana University, May 4, 1938

According to custom, those who are invited to attend the celebrations of a university are usually men or women who have attained eminence in scholarship. I come to you today with no such distinction. I did, indeed, graduate from Indiana, but I am afraid that much of what I learned here I have forgotten, and since those days my life has been spent in the market place, entirely remote from academic cloisters.

The question may well arise, therefore, as to why I am here at all. I am certainly not here because I like to speak. And I am certainly not here because I think you like to hear me speak. Frankly, the real reason I come back is because I haven't been back to an academic function since I graduated twenty-five years ago, and I have now a very keen interest in finding out what has been happening on this campus in the past twenty-five years.

In the world at large a great deal has happened during this period.

Source: Wendell L. Willkie Papers, Lilly Library, Indiana University, Bloomington.

In fact, I don't believe you could find another quarter century in history so packed with momentous events in the life of mankind. For example, we have lived through a world war in this twenty-five-year period. We have lived through one major depression and two minor ones. We have seen the governments of at least half the people in the world drastically altered in character. We have witnessed the development of half a dozen big industries, several of which—the automobile, the radio and the airplane—have had a major effect on the way we live. We have seen the social customs of a hundred years' standing rejected by a generation that wanted to make its own rules.

On the basis of these considerations, you may be expecting me to say that at the end of these twenty-five years I find the world very greatly changed. As a matter of fact, although there has been considerable rearrangement of men, methods and masters, fundamentally, I don't think we have changed very much. Whether for good or for ill, the principles by which men live remain the same as when I sat where you are sitting and heard someone tell me that I and my classmates were the hope of the world.

As one gets older, one becomes a little skeptical about the quick reforms that are designed to create the perfect state in a short period of time. We are continually tempted by catchwords to think of nations standing at the crossroads, with their fate depending on which road they choose. But the destiny of mankind is neither as simple nor as fragile as that. I cannot tell you how many "new worlds" we have been building in these twenty-five years, for example, nor have I time to enumerate the many "grave crises" the world has managed to survive. Any man who has lived through this quarter century is apt to develop a certain immunity, like that of the adult world toward measles, to the crises, cataclysms and catastrophes which we are called upon to face every year.

The last war, of course, was "the greatest in history," and so was the depression, and so was the boom period. A dozen times, I am sure, we were warned of "a great moral breakdown in the character of our people," and a revolution to be led by one group or another has been at our doors off and on many times. According to commentators both here and abroad, we have witnessed "the collapse of democracy," just about as often as we have witnessed "the downfall of the capitalist system." New Deals and New Freedoms, Red perils and the iron hand of militarism have confronted us day in and day out, and we have managed to carry on.

One of the things you will learn in your careers is that the world has a habit of emerging from soul-shattering conflicts with its soul still unshattered. I suspect that the campus of this University has maintained a similar basic immutability amid the excitements of the past twenty-five years. Frankly, I don't expect it to be very different, and I don't expect that you are any more heroic or less heroic than the young men and women who sat here twenty-five years ago.

In other words, I don't think you are a lost generation any more than you are a saved one. I don't think the world will stand or fall depending upon what your decisions in life may be. The world is a pretty tough organization, and even if this year's graduates from the University of Indiana should embark on careers of assault and battery, the world would, I think, be able to shake off your depredations without any very great harm. Similarly, if every one of you should carry a sword as fearless and honorable as Galahad's, I doubt if the world would thereupon enter the millennium.

If I should make a careful inspection of the University, therefore, after this lapse of twenty-five years, I should undoubtedly find, in addition to the new buildings, some new maps in the geographies, some new chapters in the histories, some new courses never heard of in my time, some new activities on the campus, some new customs. But I should be very much surprised if I found that your outlook on the world that lay outside these things was very different from mine. Even if I happen to have lost touch with the substance of the University, I do not think I have lost touch with its spirit.

I am aware that the phrase "the spirit of an institution" is a vague one, and I should like to define what I mean by it. I would say that the outstanding characteristic of the spirit of Indiana was—and, I think, still is—its liberalism.

We have heard a great deal about liberalism in recent years, which is a pretty good sign that the people are a little concerned about it. Just as we don't talk much about bread and water unless we foresee a scarcity, so we are apt to take liberalism for granted until it shows signs of disappearing. In Europe several of the major countries have very frankly decided that liberalism isn't worth it. And even in America we have bandied the word about rather loosely until it has lost some of its meaning and has vague political implications.

Of course, liberalism is not the property of any one political party nor the product of any one political platform. It is not a fixed program of action nor a vote on this or that particular measure. *Liberalism is an attitude of mind.* The liberal, for example, might be opposed to regulation of business in one instance and in favor of it in another. The criterion of the liberal philosophy is this: in the faith of the liberal the emphasis is upon individual freedom, while in the ideologies of either the Right or Left it is upon social control.

You can make out quite a case for social control. Mussolini and Hitler have apparently convinced their people that it is desirable. You can say that a democracy which permits too much individual freedom moves too slowly. There are a number of people who are willing to sacrifice their freedom for the sake of what they believe will be greater efficiency and prosperity. Personally, I am convinced that there is no possibility for continuing prosperity for the great mass of people except in a free political society and under a free, if supervised economy. Perhaps this is wrong, but even so, in the words of Newton Baker, "there are still many who would prefer to be poor, if necessary, but, in any case, free."

The liberal movement therefore strikes at the forces of autocracy whether they bear the label of business or government or society. It may thus be opposed to a business program at one time, and to a government program at another. And nothing illustrates this more effectively than the parallel between the liberal movement when I was your age and the true liberal movement today.

Those of you who are undergraduates will not recall the liberal movement of the first fifteen years of this century which was in full tide at the time I was in college. I can assure you, however, that the cause was an exciting one. As undergraduates we were certainly as much interested in it as you may be interested in current political and economic trends.

The early twentieth century represented the period in which the great industrial organizations reached their fullest development and influence. Gigantic combines had been built in Banking, in Oil, in

Tobacco, in Steel, in Meat Packing and in other industries. In particular, the railroads, which by that time covered the continent, were the representatives of enormous financial power.

In the development of many of these industries political influence had played an important part. The big corporation worked through political bosses in obtaining favorable government decisions. To a degree which we have never witnessed since, American business not only participated in the people's government, but frequently played a dominant part therein.

By their political power the industries of the East were able to get the franchises they wanted, to establish monopolies, to control legislation, to fatten themselves on high tariffs at the expense of the agricultural West and the South.

It is not surprising that the American people began to resent this corporate supremacy over government. The leading liberal publications denounced the vested corporate interests that were in control of American politics. The leading figures in national affairs began to demand freedom for the average man against big business and high finance. And the average man himself, in increasing numbers, began to think that that was a good idea.

For its leadership this movement was fortunate in getting three of the greatest of Americans—all three men of very different backgrounds, inclinations and talents—Theodore Roosevelt, Robert La Follette and Woodrow Wilson. I think we should also include in the list of those who inspired the pre-war liberal movement the name of a man from Indiana—Senator Albert J. Beveridge, who gave the keynote speech at the National Convention of the Progressive party in 1912, calling for "a representative government that represents the people," and urging his party to "battle for the actual rights of man."

Well, there is no time here to go into that long and colorful campaign which led to anti-trust prosecutions, to new legislation, to the quarrel between Roosevelt and Taft, to the split between Republicans and Progressives, to the election of Woodrow Wilson, and then came to an end with the World War.

The objectives of the movement were largely achieved. The oil trust, the tobacco trust, the beef trust and the other monopolies were dissolved. What Wilson called "the money trust" was ended by the Federal Reserve Act in 1913. The great corporate hand of the monopolies was pushed out of the State and Federal Legislatures, and the effort to re-establish popular control led to the direct election of Senators, the giving of votes to women, and the enactment of income tax legislation on the principle of adjusting the tax to the ability to pay. By 1914, in his message to Congress, Woodrow Wilson was able to state: "Our program of legislation with respect to business is now virtually complete. . . . The road at last lies clear and firm before business."

That briefly was the cause that enlisted the enthusiasm of the liberals of my time—the cause of the people against corporate domination. Perhaps if there had not been a war, the road would have remained clear for business. But the war gave to business all over the world the highly artificial character of a war activity, and the governments of the world took control of business in order to administer it for military purposes.

The moral and economic dislocation thus caused by the war must be regarded as a primary cause for the extravagant speculation, the abuse of industrial power, the neglect of industrial trusteeship that followed it. By the time the depression crept like a cloud over the world, the people had plenty of abuses to charge against industry and plenty of argument for government regulation. In a desperate haste to achieve reforms they turned more and more to the government to run their affairs. In Germany, Italy and Russia the power given to the government is today complete. In England, France, Canada and the United States the people still retain the ultimate power, but have encouraged the government to assume more and more responsibility for their jobs, their health, their old age, their security.

The cause of liberalism today, therefore, has changed. In the prewar years we fought against domination of the people by Big Business. We now face the domination of the people by Big Government. I am not speaking of the United States alone, but of the trend which is apparent thoroughout the world. The liberal who fought against one kind of domination thirty-five years ago should find himself fighting against this new kind of domination today.

The liberal will, of course, be sympathetic with the principles of much of the social legislation of recent years, but the liberal will also be on his guard lest this trend go too far and suppress the individualism and initiative which are the basic factors in the continuing advance of any civilization.

Remember that almost every time you have a necessarily complex law regulating an industry nowadays, you must set up a commission to administer it. We started with the Interstate Commerce Commission in 1887 and gave it new powers under Theodore Roosevelt in 1906. Then we had the Federal Trade Commission and the Federal Power Commission under Woodrow Wilson, and expanded the Federal Power Commission under Hoover. Since then, we have rapidly added others; the Securities and Exchange Commission which controls security issues and security markets; the Federal Communications Commission with control over broadcasting, telephoning and telegraphing; the National Labor Relations Board, which controls the labor relations of industry; the Bituminous Coal Commission, which can set both prices and wages in the bituminous coal industry; the Agricultural Adjustment Administration to carry out the changing provisions of the agricultural acts; and dozens of others.

No believer in true democracy can view this trend toward a commission form of government without alarm. As the Government has extended its control over industry, it has transferred exercise of that control to commissions which establish the rules whereby that industry should be conducted. In other words, the rules are not fixed by the Legislature, but by the Commission; they may fluctuate with the Commission's personnel. Thus we have a highly personal form of government—a government of men, instead of a government of laws—in which the favor of a commission chairman determines the conduct of an industry that may be employing several hundred thousand people and owned by several million stockholders.

For example, it is not the Securities Act which tells a corporation what it must do with respect to the sale of its securities and it is not the Securities Exchange Act which tells the Stock Exchanges what they must do with respect to the securities traded in their markets. In both instances, one must look, not to the law, but to the Commission to find out what the requirements are. And it is not the

Wagner Act which can guide a corporation in forming its industrial relations program. It is the National Labor Relations Board. No broadcasting station can read the law governing broadcasting and find out what rules it must observe. It has to consult with the Federal Communication Commission.

So numerous are the departments, bureaus and commissions of all kinds now dominating the life of America that a year or so ago the United States Government began issuing an annual special directory for the guidance of the public. It names and describes eighty-two such departments and agencies, affecting almost every factor in the nation's life. We have more than one million Federal office holders—not including any State office holders—and at the last count they were increasing at the rate of one hundred an hour a month or so ago. The salary list of the Federal Government now amounts to billions of dollars a year.

In number of employees, in salary payments, in annual budget, in scope of activities, here is the greatest corporation in the world. This corporation has what you might call a regular operating budget of about $3,332,000,000, but it has a special budget of perhaps four billion dollars a year for public works, for unemployment relief, for agriculture.

The existence of Big Government on such a scale represents as much of a test of the true liberalism as did Big Business twenty-five years ago. The true liberal is as much opposed to excessive concentration of power in the hands of government as to excessive concentration of power in the hands of business. In other words, he maintains his freedom against all comers.

For example, in the period before the War, certain industries in the East grew fat on high tariffs. The liberal was opposed to these high tariffs because they were little more than subsidies given to a favored few. Likewise, today the liberal is opposed to subsidies given by the government to its own agencies for the purpose of competing with the people's business.

In the period before the War it was intolerable to the liberal that the corporation counsel of a railroad or manufacturer should have secret access to the Judge's chamber. Today, the liberal must condemn with equal vigor the statement by the present Solicitor General of the United States that, as Assistant Attorney General, he did his best to take his government cases to "a friendly court."

The true liberal would not tolerate such a thing as corporate efforts to influence the courts before the War. He will not tolerate executive or legislative domination of the courts today.

To the true liberal the attempt on the part of corporations to control legislatures was abhorent. It must be equally abhorrent to him that a government should use for political purposes the enormous sums appropriated for relief.

The true liberal before the War was opposed to the efforts on the part of corporations to prevent their employees from organizing. And the true liberal today must be equally outraged when the government permits the Mayor of Jersey City to throw union organizers in jail—or eject socialists from the town—merely because the Mayor of Jersey City is Vice Chairman of the National Democratic Committee.

The true liberals today face exactly the same type of enemy under a different name that the liberals faced in the first fifteen years of this century. The difference is that the fight on behalf of liberalism in our time has become all the more important because liberalism has lost in perhaps half of the territory of the world.

When I was an undergraduate in Indiana, there were many nations under an autocratic form of government—many nations in which the rights of the people were respected either not at all or very little. But the trend at that time was toward freedom. Each year the people marched a little further ahead toward that goal. Then the War came, and for a short time freedom seemed to have won a victory. Old monarchies were destroyed. Territories were rearranged. Some half dozen countries were put on the map which were not on the map in the University of my day. We even were arguing pro and con the advantages of a new principle in democracy—a democracy of nations, which would offer a method whereby the nations could settle their disputes in peace rather than by resort to war.

As I say, the trend was toward freedom; but today the trend has been reversed. At that time the institutions of monarchy and absolute control were under question. Today the institutions of democracy and individual liberty are under question. Mussolini, Hitler and Stalin believe the democratic form of government to be obsolete; they are convinced that their governments are far superior. They deprecate the cause of peace, maintaining that war offers certain advantages. They are opposed to free speech and a free press, claiming that censorship is for the good of the people.

If you are anxious to preserve the American system, therefore, you must be aware of the fact that there are those from outside who expect it to be destroyed and who will be glad to lend a hand in its destroying. "The struggle between the two worlds can have no compromise," states Mussolini. "Either We or They. Either their ideas or ours. Either our state or theirs."

If it is a question of either "We or They" certainly what "They" have does not compare, in all fairness, with what "We" still retain. We manage to pay our workers more, charge the consumer less, and make a better product than the manufacturers of any European country. Despite all the difficulties of recent years, we still have by far the highest standard of living; not only the highest in material comforts, but the highest in spiritual possessions; not only better machines, but more freedom. And we have achieved this because we have maintained the system of free enterprise under a Democratic Government. The surrender of liberalism to the theory of the totalitarian state would mean the sacrifice of the free man's achievement for a regulated and second-rate society.

So, just as I left the University of Indiana twenty-five years ago, sworn to defend the liberal cause, I return to it today pledged to the same purpose. The liberal cause is still in need of defense. I do not doubt that you will defend it. You could hardly spend four years here in this university, in this state, without absorbing a faith in the rights of man. Perhaps I should warn you, however, that liberalism is neither easy nor sensational. Very rarely is it called upon to storm the barricades with flags waving, and very rarely can it rely simply upon a good heart to determine the merits of its cause. Frequently you will find yourself in the minority, and sometimes you will find yourself alone.

In fact, the liberal attempts to do the most difficult thing in the world—namely, to strike a true balance between the rights of the individual and the needs of society. He is like a man rowing a boat who, when the boat swings to the right pulls on the left, and when it swings to left, pulls on the right. Liberalism sticks to the middle of the road, speaks quietly and insists upon the color of no man's shirt. If its voice seems small in the present tumult of shouting—if its ranks seem thinned among the regiments in uniform—let that be a sign to you, who have been educated in its spirit, to recognize the urgency of its cause.

BIBLIOGRAPHIC ESSAY

Two general biographies of Wendell Willkie provide good starting points for understanding his life. Ellsworth Barnard, *Wendell Willkie: Fighter for Freedom* (Marquette, Mich., 1966), is the more detailed, with the added advantage of being based on the author's interviews and correspondence with Willkie family members and associates. Steve Neal, *Dark Horse: A Biography of Wendell Willkie* (Garden City, N.Y., 1984), is a well-written narrative, available in paperback.

Other books treat Willkie from a variety of approaches. A sympathetic and moving account is provided in *Willkie* (New York, 1952) by Joseph Barnes, a journalist friend who accompanied Willkie on his world trip. His early life is treated with some insight and some fiction in Alden Hatch, *Young Willkie* (New York, 1944). An interesting literary and poetic presentation is Muriel Rukeyser, *One Life* (New York, 1957). Less sympathetic is Mary Earhart Dillon, *Wendell Willkie, 1892–1944* (New York, 1952).

Among several interesting essays are Roscoe Drummond, "Wendell Willkie: A Study in Courage," in Isabel Leighton, ed., *The Aspirin Age, 1919–1941* (New York, 1949); Janet Flanner, "Rushville's Renowned Son-in-Law," *New Yorker,* October 12, 1940, 27–42; Elizabeth R. Valentine, "A Defeated Candidate Remains a Leader," *New York Times Magazine,* June 1, 1941; Norman Cousins, "Mr. Willkie," *Saturday Review of Literature,* October 14, 1944; and John Morton Blum's account in *V Was for Victory: Politics and American Culture during World War II* (New York, 1976). A recent memoir by the young lawyer who organized the Associated Willkie Clubs in 1940 is Oren Root, "Why We Wanted Willkie," *Constitution,* Spring/Summer 1990, 50–58.

Studies of the political environment in which Willkie worked include Donald B. Johnson, *The Republican Party and Wendell Willkie* (Urbana, Ill.,

1960); Warren Moscow, *Roosevelt and Willkie* (Englewood Cliffs, N.J., 1968); Herbert S. Parmet and Marie B. Hecht, *Never Again: A President Runs for a Third Term* (New York, 1968); Hugh Ross, "Was the Nomination of Wendell Willkie a Political Miracle?" *Indiana Magazine of History*, June 1962, 79–100; Ross Gregory, "Politics in an Age of Crisis: America, and Indiana, in the Election of 1940," *Indiana Magazine of History*, September 1990, 247–80; R. J. C. Butow, "The FDR Tapes," *American Heritage*, February/March 1982; and James MacGregor Burns, *Roosevelt: The Soldier of Freedom* (New York, 1970).

The international context for Willkie's views is given in Robert A. Divine, *The Reluctant Belligerent: American Entry into World War II*, 2d ed. (New York, 1979); Robert Divine, *Foreign Policy and U.S. Presidential Elections, 1940–1948* (New York, 1974); Robert Dallek, *Franklin D. Roosevelt and American Foreign Policy, 1932–1945* (New York, 1979); Wayne S. Cole, *Roosevelt and the Isolationists, 1932–1945* (Lincoln, Nebr., 1983); and James C. Schneider, *Should America Go to War? The Debate over Foreign Policy in Chicago, 1939–1941* (Chapel Hill, N. C., 1989).

Background for understanding Willkie's support of civil rights and civil liberties can be found in John B. Kirby, *Black Americans in the Roosevelt Era: Liberalism and Race* (Knoxville, Tenn., 1980); Clayton R. Koppes and Gregory D. Black, *Hollywood Goes to War: How Politics, Profits, and Propaganda Shaped World War II Movies* (New York, 1987); Samuel Walker, *In Defense of American Liberties* (New York, 1990); and Neil A. Wynn, *The Afro-American and the Second World War* (New York, 1975).

Essential to understanding Willkie's thought and appeal are his own published writings. *One World* (New York, 1943), Willkie's best-selling account of his 1942 global tour, contains his perspectives on colonialism and the interdependence of America's domestic and foreign policy, especially on matters of race. Also important is *An American Program* (New York, 1944), published just before his death. Some of his earlier publications and speeches are gathered in *This Is Wendell Willkie* (New York, 1940). *New Republic, Saturday Evening Post, Collier's,* and other periodical magazines of the early 1940s contain numerous articles by Willkie.

The most important collection of primary sources is the Wendell Willkie Papers at the Lilly Library, Indiana University, Bloomington. The papers, relating primarily to his political activities from 1939 to 1944, include ninety-eight cartons of correspondence, nine cartons of speeches and writings, seventeen cartons of newspaper clippings, and thirteen shelves of scrapbooks. There also are several hundred photographs. Also at the Lilly Library are the papers of the Willkie Clubs of America and the papers of Willkie biographer Ellsworth Barnard. At the Library of Congress, Washington, D.C., the papers of Irita Van Doren contain large amounts of important Willkie material.

WENDELL WILLKIE
CHRONOLOGY

February 18, 1892	Birth, Elwood, Indiana
June 1913	Graduation from Indiana University
September, 1913–November, 1914	High school history teacher, Coffeyville, Kansas
June 1916	Law degree, Indiana University
1917–1919	Army service, World War I
January 14, 1918	Marriage to Edith Wilk
December 7, 1919	Birth of son, Philip
1919–1929	Lawyer, Akron, Ohio
1929	Begins law practice, New York City
1933–1940	President, Commonwealth and Southern, and New Deal critic
June 28, 1940	Wins Republican nomination for president
August 17, 1940	Acceptance ceremonies, Elwood, Indiana
November 5, 1940	Loss in presidential election to Franklin D. Roosevelt
January–February, 1941	Visit to war-torn England
February 11, 1941	Testimony in support of Lend-Lease
July 19, 1942	Address to NAACP

August 26– October 14, 1942	Trip around the world
November 9, 1942	Pleads Schneiderman case before Supreme Court
April, 1943	*One World* published
April 4, 1944	Defeat in Wisconsin presidential primary
October 7, 1944	Publication of *An American Program*
October 8, 1944	Death in New York City, burial later in Rushville, Indiana

CONTRIBUTORS

GEORGE T. BLAKEY, Professor of History, Indiana University East in Richmond, earned degrees from Berea College, Vanderbilt University, and Indiana University. His recent publications include *Hard Times and New Deal in Kentucky* (1986) and "Esther G. White: Awakener of Hoosier Potential," *Indiana Magazine of History,* September 1990.

ROSS GREGORY, a graduate of Indiana University (Ph.D., 1964), is Professor of History, Western Michigan University. His publications include *Walter Hines Page,* which won the Frederick Jackson Turner Prize of the Organization of American Historians, *American Intervention in the First World War,* and *America 1941: A Nation at the Crossroads.*

HOWARD JONES is University Research Professor of History at the University of Alabama. He is the author of several books, including *Munity on the Amistad: The Saga of A Slave Revolt and Its Impact on American Abolition, Law, and Diplomacy* (1987), *The Course of American Diplomacy: From the Revolution to the Present* (1988), *"A New Kind of War": America's Global Strategy and the Truman Doctrine in Greece* (1989), and, with Randall B. Woods, *Dawning of the Cold War: The United States' Quest for Order* (1991).

ANDRÉ KASPI is Professor of North American History at the Sorbonne (Université de Paris I), where he heads the Centre d'histoire nord-américaine. He has taught as visiting professor in several American universities. His doctoral thesis, *Le Temps des Américains* (1976), addresses Franco-American relations in 1917–1918. Among his publications are *Les Américains: Les Etats-Unis de 1607 à nos jours* (1988), and *Franklin Roosevelt* (1988).

MARK H. LEFF is Associate Professor of American History at the University of Illinois, Urbana-Champaign. His studies of economic policymaking in the 1930s and 1940s include *The Limits of Symbolic Reform* (1984) and "The Politics of Sacrifice on the American Home Front in World War II," *Journal of American History*, March 1991.

JAMES H. MADISON is Professor of History at Indiana University, Bloomington, and editor of the *Indiana Magazine of History*. Among his books are *Indiana through Tradition and Change: A History of the Hoosier State and Its People, 1920–1945* (1982), *The Indiana Way: A State History* (1986), *Eli Lilly: A Life, 1885–1977* (1989), and, as editor, *Heartland: Comparative Histories of the Midwestern States* (1988).

ALEXANDER S. MANYKIN is Senior Research Fellow, Department of Modern and Contemporary History, Moscow State University. Among his publications are *Izoliatsionizm i formirovanie vneshnepoliticheskogo kursa SShA, 1923–1929* (*Isolationism and American foreign policymaking, 1923–1929*) (1980) and *Era demokratov: Partiinaia peregruppirovka v SShA 1933–1952* (*The Democratic era: Party realignment in the U.S., 1933–1952*) (1990).

HARVARD SITKOFF is Professor of History, University of New Hampshire, and John Adams Professor of American Civilization in the Netherlands. He is the author of *A New Deal for Blacks* (1978) and *The Struggle for Black Equality* (1981), co-author of *The Enduring Vision: A History of the American People* (1990), and editor of *Fifty Years Later: The New Deal Evaluated* (1985).

INDEX

Africa: Willkie's 1942 world tour, 112

African Americans: enduring contributions of Willkie, xiii; Willkie's advocacy of racial justice, xix–xx; Willkie and 1940 presidential campaign, 74; Willkie on movie industry stereotypes, 75, 79. *See also* Civil rights

Agricultural Adjustment Administration: Willkie on government regulation of business, 163

Akron, Ohio: Willkie and urbanism, 6

American Bar Association: Willkie as member of Committee on the Bill of Rights, 76

American Hebrew medal: Willkie on civil rights and liberties, 79

American Liberty League: New Deal and liberalism, 37

An American Program: Willkie as a writer, 18; Willkie on racial justice, 84; Willkie and internationalism, 117–18; Republican party foreign policy agenda, 152

Anti-Semitism: Willkie and civil rights, 76, 78. *See also* Holocaust

Armed forces: Willkie on civil rights, 79

Associated Press: Willkie's 1941 trip to England, 108

Baker, Newton D.: Willkie's admiration of Woodrow Wilson, 49; on freedom and economics, 160

Baltimore Afro-American: support of Willkie in 1940 elections, 74

Barnes, Joseph: on public response to Willkie's death, xx; on Willkie as a writer, 17; Willkie's 1942 world tour, 112

Battle of Britain: Willkie and foreign policy, 61

Beveridge, Albert: Indiana tradition of oratory, 12; prewar liberal movement, 161

Bituminous Coal Commission: Willkie on government regulation of business, 163

Black Committee: public utilities and lobbying abuses, 27

Blakey, George T.: influence on Willkie of Indiana background, xiv

Blum, Léon: French relations with U.S. in 1930s, 126

Bridges, Harry: Willkie and Supreme Court ruling on Schneiderman case, 77

Bright, Jesse: independence of Hoosier politicians, 8–9

Browder, Earl: Willkie on civil liberties, 73

Bryan, William Jennings: Willkie and oratory, 12; Willkie and term *loyal opposition*, 121

Bryan, William Lowe: presidential campaign of 1940 and Willkie's association with Indiana University, ix; eulogy for Willkie at Indiana University, x

Burns, James MacGregor: relationship between Roosevelt and Willkie, xix

Burton, Harold: Republican foreign policy and shift away from isolationism, 152

Business: Willkie and progressivism, 48; two sides of Willkie's political thought at end of 1930s, 51. *See also* Industry; Public utilities